Voices & Votes
How Democracy Works in Wisconsin

Jonathan Kasparek
Bobbie Malone

Wisconsin Historical Society Press

Published by the Wisconsin Historical Society Press
© 2005 by the State Historical Society of Wisconsin

www.wisconsinhistory.org/whspress

Photographs identified with PH, WHi, or WHS are from the Society's collections; address inquiries about such photos to the Visual Materials Archivist at the above address.

Publications of the Wisconsin Historical Society Press are available at quantity discounts for promotions, fund raising, and educational use. Write to the above address for more information.

Printed in Canada

Cover and text design by Jill Bremigan

09 08 07 06 05   1 2 3 4 5

Library of Congress Cataloging-in-Publication Data

Kasparek, Jon.
   Voices & votes : how democracy works in Wisconsin / Jonathan Kasparek, Bobbie Malone.
      p. cm.
   Includes bibliographical references and index.
   ISBN 0-87020-363-0 (alk. paper)
   1. Wisconsin--Politics and government--1951--Textbooks. I. Title: Voices and votes. II. Malone, Bobbie, 1944- III. Title.
   JK6016.K37 2005
   320.4775--dc22

                                                                    2005015106

**Other Titles in the
New Badger History Series**
(Includes classroom texts and teacher guides)

*Digging and Discovery:
Wisconsin Archaeology*

*Learning from the Land:
Wisconsin Land Use*

Working with Water: Wisconsin Waterways

They Came to Wisconsin

Native People of Wisconsin

Front cover: Photo courtesy of Madison Newspapers, Inc.

∞ The paper used in this publication meets the minimum requirements of the American National Standard for Information Sciences—Permanence of Paper for Printed Library Materials, ANSI Z39.48-1992.

Voices & Votes
How Democracy Works in Wisconsin

Contents

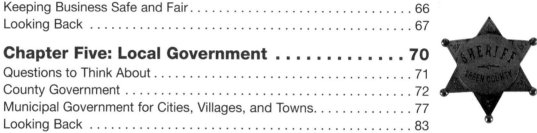

Introduction

Making Democracy Work

This is a book about something that shapes the lives of people in Wisconsin and in our country. But it's not something we think about much of the time—our government and our place in it.

What do you think of when you hear the word "government"? Perhaps you think of the president of the United States in our nation's capital, Washington, D.C. Or maybe you picture the dome of the state capitol in Madison, just as you see on the cover of this book. Or perhaps you have been to your local courthouse or police station. Government is really all these things . . . and much more.

Wouldn't it be nice if you were always first in line? Wouldn't you like to have your choice of any seat at the movies or on the school bus? The problem is, everybody else would like the same thing. How do we decide a fair way to make decisions that affect lots of people? That's what government is; people working *together* to make rules to keep things fair and safe. One person cannot build roads or highways or run a fire department, so government is both the people who **enforce** the rules and also the people who do things like plowing snow and delivering mail.

And we in Wisconsin and in our country live under a special kind of government known as a **democracy** (dih **mok** ruh see). In a democracy, we choose our own leaders, people who **represent** (reh pre **zent**) or speak for us in government. Because we live in a **democratic** (dem uh **krat** ik) country, the government is really *us*.

You have probably read stories about kings and queens who rule their people. But living in a democracy means that we live in a country where the people rule or govern themselves. The "voices" you see in the title of this book belong to the people in our democracy.

enforce: To make sure that a rule or law is obeyed   **democratic:** Where people choose their own leaders to represent them

How do people make their voices heard in a democracy? They do it by electing their own leaders to represent them. That's why "votes" is also in the title of this book.

Democracy always involves 2 ideas: rights and **responsibilities** (rih spon suh **bil** uh teez). Democracy gives people the *right* to govern themselves. And then people have the *responsibility* to exercise or use that right by voting. Every election gives people the opportunity to have a voice in the kind of government they want. People choose who will be president of the United States, who will represent them in state government, and even who serves on the local school board.

The government is supposed to work in the best interests of everybody, even though not everyone can vote. For example, children don't vote. When parents vote, they represent their children. Yet, children are still part of the people of Wisconsin.

And in this book, you'll discover that in the years since Wisconsin became a state, more and more adults have been given the right to vote. That's just one of the ways our democracy has changed.

You might wonder exactly what all of this means to you, since it will be many years before you can vote. *Voices & Votes* is something like a tool kit. It will give you lots of information. After reading this book, you'll know how government works. You'll find out about many kinds of government in Wisconsin. You'll learn that different levels of government do different things. You'll see how government has changed over time. And most important, you'll get ideas about what you *can* do, *even before you can vote,* to make democracy in Wisconsin work better for all those who live here, now and in the future.

responsibilities: Duties or jobs

Chapter 1

How Does Government Work?

★ ★ ★

How do rules at school and rules from the government make life fair and safe?

Do you have to follow a lot of rules at your school? Do you raise your hand before talking in class? Or maybe you have to stand in line at the drinking fountain instead of pushing ahead? Sometimes it is hard to follow all these rules, but they are there for good reasons.

Since lots of students want to talk in class, you raise your hand so that everyone can have a turn. Since it is dangerous to push and shove in the hallway, standing in line keeps you safe. It's difficult to be heard when everyone is yelling during the lunch break, so each person speaks in a normal voice. These rules make it fair for everyone.

Government does the same things—people get together to make the rules to make life fairer and to keep people safe. In a democracy, everyone has a voice in making these rules, which become laws. Then everyone has to follow them. In this chapter, you'll learn many things about the different forms of government that people live under in our American democracy.

2

Questions to Think About

How does government work? Why is it important to know how government works? How does democracy in Wisconsin work? Why is the state capital in Madison? What's the difference between state government and national government? Who really makes decisions about how government works? What kind of governments do Wisconsin Indian Nations have?

WHi Image ID 19029

Policeman directing traffic in Madison in 1931

3

Government Has Different Levels

The levels of government in the United States

Graphic by Amelia Janes,
Midwest Educational Graphics

Now you know a little about what government is and what it does. But did you know that there are actually different levels of government?

One level of government is **federal** (**fed** ur uhl). In a federal government like that of the United States of America, Wisconsin and all the other states are united under and controlled by one government. We recognize Washington, D.C., as our nation's capital. But in a federal system, each state has its own government and can make its own laws.

The United States is one of more than 200 different nations in the world. Federal governments like ours are also **sovereign** (**sahv** rihn). Sovereign means that a nation has the right to **govern** itself.

Our federal government is headed by the president, who lives in the White House in Washington, D.C. You have probably seen the president on television or in the newspaper. The people of the United States send **representatives** (reh pre **zen** tuh tivs) to **Congress** (**cong** griss). Congress is the part of our federal government where laws are made. Laws are rules that everyone in the United States has to follow. Because the United States is a democracy, voters decide who will be president and who will represent them in Congress.

Most U.S. presidents, such as Abraham Lincoln, have lived in the White House.

WHi Image ID 23605

4   **govern:** To rule   **representatives:** People chosen to speak or act for others

The United States of America is a nation made up of 50 states. The 13 original states that decided to form the United States were independent. They had to decide how much of their power to give up to the new federal government. The states kept some power, gave some to the federal government, and reserved much for the people.

We live in Wisconsin, a state located in the north-central part of the United States. People in each state have to obey the laws of the United States. But in other ways, the states also govern themselves. Each state has the right to set speed limits on roads and highways, for example. And each state can decide how many students should be in classrooms at different grade levels.

People in Wisconsin make their own laws by sending representatives from their areas to a state **legislature** (**lej** uh sla tschur) in Madison. A legislature is an elected group of people who have the power to make laws for the state. These lawmakers are known as **legislators** (**lej** uh sla turz). They are elected by their neighbors to make laws for the state.

The head of the state government is the governor, who is also elected by all the voters in the state. The legislature and the governor can make and enforce laws *only* in Wisconsin. They cannot make laws for the people of

Legislators discuss laws at the Capitol.

Minnesota or Illinois. Each state is independent of all other states in making certain decisions about its government. On some decisions, states have no independent say.

This may be confusing, but think about how your school works. You live in a school district that includes elementary schools, middle schools, and high schools. Each school district is headed by a school board and a superintendent. They are something like the federal government. That is, the school board and superintendent make rules that every school in the district must follow. For example, every school must have classes for the same number of days each year. Every school must have certain days off, like Saturdays, Sundays, and holidays.

But each school in your school district can also make its own rules. Your school is headed by a principal, who makes rules that the teachers and students in your school must follow. Your school's day might begin at a different time from the high school. Your school might have a different time for recess than another school.

Other schools do not have to follow your principal's rules because they have their own principals and their own rules. The high school might have a longer day of classes and no recess. Schools in a school district are like states in our nation. They all have to follow the district's rules, but they can make their own, too.

THE WISCONSIN STATE CAPITAL AND CAPITOL

When "capital" is spelled with an "a," it means the city that is home to the government. When "capitol" is spelled with an "o," it refers to the building that houses government. Wisconsin's first capital was Belmont in 1836, and its second capital was Burlington (now in Iowa) in 1837 and 1838. Madison has been the *capital* of Wisconsin since 1838, but the *capitol* building has changed many times.

The first capitol in Madison was a small stone building with a shallow dome. When the representatives first met there in the winter of 1838, they found the building unfinished and freezing. Pigs were kept in the basement! Between 1857 and 1868, the state built a larger stone building.

The state government quickly outgrew the building, and 2 wings were added in 1881. Then a fire mostly destroyed the capitol. Between 1906 and 1917, the state built the capitol you see in Madison today. The capitol is built of white granite and filled with colorful marble and works of art. Our capitol is one of the most beautiful in the country, and it has one of the largest domes in the world.

This building in Belmont was used as the first Wisconsin Territorial Capitol in 1836 and is now a historic site you can visit.

The second Wisconsin Capitol was built in Madison, but by 1857 government had outgrown it.

The third Wisconsin Capitol was destroyed in a fire on February 27, 1904.

Today, when you visit Madison, you can see one of the most beautiful capitol buildings in the country!

Left to right: WHi Image ID 10476; WHi Image 3965; WHi Image ID 9562; Kathleen Sitter, Legislative Reference Bureau

The governments of the 50 states make up part of the government of the United States of America. Wisconsin is made up of many smaller governments. These smaller governments are local governments and make up the third level of government. This third, local level of government includes counties, cities, villages, and towns. There are 72 counties and nearly 2,000 cities, towns, and villages in Wisconsin. All of these local governments have to follow the laws of Wisconsin, but they can also make laws for themselves. For example, a city might enforce speed limits on its streets to keep people safe. Or a county might run a snowplow service to clear the highways during the winter.

Think about how your school works. Local governments are like your school's classrooms. Each classroom has to follow the rules set by the school district and the principal, but your classroom can make its own rules. Perhaps you

Today these 72 counties shown on this map make up the state of Wisconsin.

8

have math class at a certain time each day. Or your teacher has a rule about using the pencil sharpener. Another classroom may decide to do these things very differently.

Why Do We Have to Have All These Levels of Government?

It may be difficult to sort out what each level of government does. You might be wondering: Why can't we just have a federal level? Wouldn't that be easier? Actually, each level of government has different responsibilities. First, it is more **efficient** (uh **fish** unt) to make some decisions at the local level. Can you imagine the president having to decide every morning in the winter which schools should be closed because of snowstorms? Even the governor in Madison may not be able to decide whether schools in Oshkosh should close.

A rural mail carrier loading his car with mail sacks in Madison, 1934

There are very good reasons to have separate levels of government. The federal government protects us from other countries, but it cannot run the police department in every city. The federal government also has to deal with big issues that affect everybody in the United States. For example, the federal government provides federal services like delivering the mail. Imagine how confusing it would be if every state issued its own postage stamps or charged different rates to mail a letter or package!

efficient: To work without wasting time

9

The DNR works hard to protect our natural resources so we can all enjoy them.

States deal with smaller issues. Among other things, Wisconsin manages state highways and runs the University of Wisconsin system to provide higher-level education. The state also protects its environment through the Department of Natural Resources (DNR). And the state operates a court system to keep the peace.

Local governments also have responsibilities. The state cannot plow everyone's streets during the winter, so the county or city does it. Each village or city provides its own police and fire departments.

Second, different levels of government allow more freedom for people to do what they want. For example, if the people of a city really like swimming, the city can open a public swimming pool in one of its parks. People living in another city might not like swimming as much as they like playing tennis. In one of its parks, this city can open a public tennis court. Imagine how unhappy this second city would be if the state or federal government made them build a swimming pool instead of a tennis court.

With different levels of government, each city or state can choose for itself. If the people of Wisconsin decide to build a new state highway they can, even if other states do not think they need any new highways. Each state can do what it wants. Both state and local governments can decide to do different things based on what is best for the people who live there.

Together, these 3 levels of government allow people to govern themselves through the leaders they elect. Those adults who live in a city elect a mayor and city council to make laws for the city. People in a state elect a governor and legislature to make laws for the state. People in the United States elect a president and Congress to make laws for the entire nation.

WHi (X3) 26103

Local governments protect their citizens by providing a police force, such as this one from long ago in Kaukauna.

Tribal Governments

Two hundred years ago, all of Wisconsin belonged to several American Indian Nations. The Menominee lived in the northeast. The Ojibwe lived in the north. The Potawatomi lived in the Milwaukee area, and the Ho-Chunk lived in the western and central part of the state. Other tribes, like the Dakota, the Mesquakie (meh **skwah** kee), and the Sauk also lived in Wisconsin at that time. Like the original 13 American colonies, all of these Nations are sovereign. Indian Nations today have their own governments and make their own laws independently of one another, just as they did in the past.

Long before Europeans came to North America, each Indian Nation developed its own way of governing itself. Leaders led by the **consent** (cun **sent**) of the people, which meant they had to get tribal members to agree with them.

Native American treaty lands, 1825

LAKE SUPERIOR

Ojibwe

Green Bay

Menominee

Dakota

Mississippi River

LAKE MICHIGAN

Ho-Chunk

Ojibwe

Sauk and Meskwaki (Sauk and Fox)

Potawatomi

Potawatomi

----- Modern state borders

During the 1800s, Europeans and Euro-Americans began to move to Wisconsin. The Indian Nations held the land, but the U.S. government had more power. Because the Indian Nations are also sovereign, they entered into **treaties** with the federal government. These American Indians were forced to **cede** (seed), or give up, their land to the federal government. The government, in turn, sold the land to the new, non-Indian settlers.

With the arrival of more and more settlers, American Indians were forced to sign treaties with the U.S. government to cede their land. This painting shows the treaty-making at Prairie du Chien in 1825.

Although these Indian Nations ceded much of their land, some groups kept, or **reserved** (re **zervd**), a small part of that land. These areas that the Native people kept for themselves are called **reservations** (rez ur **vay** shuns).

Indian Nations never gave up certain powers that were part of their tribal sovereignty. The people on these reservations are still governed by the tribal governments, which they choose. In some ways, tribal governments are independent of the state. But in other cases, tribal governments follow both state and federal laws.

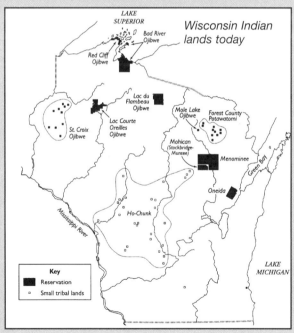

Wisconsin Indian lands today

LAKE SUPERIOR
Bad River Ojibwe
Red Cliff Ojibwe
Lac du Flambeau Ojibwe
Mole Lake Ojibwe
Forest County Potawatomi
St. Croix Ojibwe
Lac Courte Oreilles Ojibwe
Mohican (Stockbridge-Munsee)
Menominee
Green Bay
Oneida
Mississippi River
Ho-Chunk
LAKE MICHIGAN

Key
■ Reservation
□ Small tribal lands

Government Can Change

So far, you've read that different levels of government do different things. All make laws, but about different things. All provide different services that the people living in Wisconsin need. But these different levels of government have not always existed.

Many years before Wisconsin was a state, it was a **territory** (**ter** uh tor ee). A territory is a piece of land that belongs to the United States but is not a state. People living in a territory do not have the same rights as those who live in a state. There are now 50 states, and most of these states began as territories. As more people settled in a territory, they gained more control over their **territorial** (ter uh **tor** ee uhl) government and eventually became states.

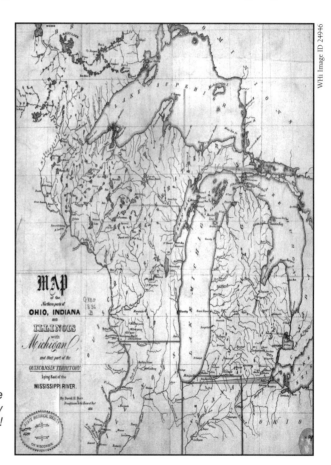

WHi Image ID 24946

This map of 1836 shows the states around Lake Michigan and Lake Superior. Wisconsin was a territory at this time. Compare it with a current map!

The U.S. Congress created the Wisconsin Territory in 1836. At first, most of the land in the territory still belonged to the American Indian Nations living there. Little by little, the federal government made treaties with the Indian Nations and took most of their land. By 1848, all of Wisconsin—except the small areas of land the Indian Nations kept for themselves—was owned by the federal government. Wisconsin was now open to settlement by American and European immigrants. These settlers were the people who formed Wisconsin's territorial government. No Native people in the area were part of that government.

The settlers in the Wisconsin Territory between 1836 and 1848 had limited say in the way they were governed. They elected representatives to a territorial assembly, which met every year to make laws for the territory. But people in the territory could not elect a governor and other officials. These leaders were appointed by the president. President Andrew Jackson appointed Henry Dodge to be Wisconsin Territory's first governor.

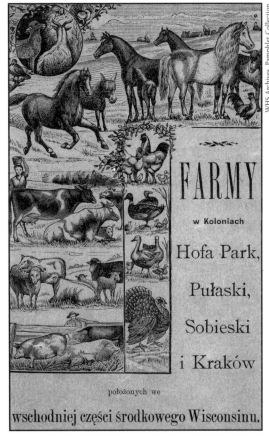

Before they came to the United States, immigrants found out more about Wisconsin from letters, books, and pamphlets, such as this one written in Polish.

HENRY DODGE AND JAMES DUANE DOTY

Two people, Henry Dodge (1782–1867) and James Duane Doty (1799–1865), were the most important leaders while Wisconsin was a territory. They had very different personalities. In 1827, Dodge moved to Mineral Point in the lead-mining region of southwestern Wisconsin. He came from Missouri with his wife and their children. Dodge had been a military leader. He led Wisconsin soldiers during the Black Hawk War of 1832. Dodge then served as territorial governor from 1836 to 1841 and from 1845 to 1848. Between 1841 and 1845, he represented Wisconsin Territory in the U.S. Congress.

James Duane Doty came to Wisconsin in 1824 as a judge for the territory. As he traveled the area on horseback and by canoe, Doty got to know the area better than anyone. He used his knowledge to make money by buying and selling land. Doty also represented the Wisconsin Territory between 1839 and 1841, and was governor from 1841 to 1845.

Dodge was a popular leader, but Doty never was. Many people thought Doty was too interested in using the territory to make money for himself. And he did. He owned much of the land that later became the capital city, Madison.

Henry Dodge, first governor of Wisconsin Territory WHi Image ID 2614

James Doty, founder of Madison, and a key leader in Wisconsin Territory

WHi Image ID 11337

The people in Wisconsin Territory did not have a say in federal government. Every state had a voice in the U.S. Congress. Each state elected representatives to the U.S. House of Representatives and **senators** to the U.S. Senate. As a territory, Wisconsin had no U.S. Senator and only one U.S. Representative who couldn't even vote in Congress.

This may seem very **undemocratic** (un dem o **krat** ik), and in a way, it was. But remember that a state was first a territory for only a short while. And territories had very few settlers. Although many Native people lived in the territory, they had no voice or vote at that time. In Chapter 6, you'll read more about why Native people could not vote.

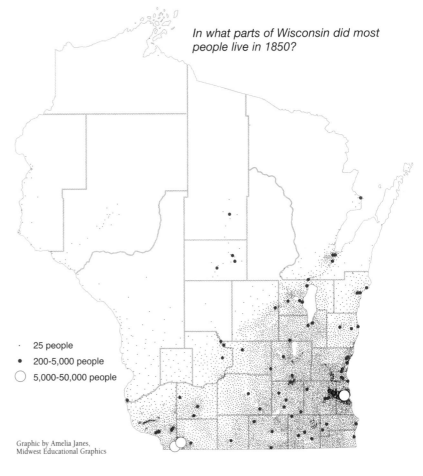

In what parts of Wisconsin did most people live in 1850?

· 25 people
• 200-5,000 people
◯ 5,000-50,000 people

Graphic by Amelia Janes,
Midwest Educational Graphics

undemocratic: Not very well representing the wishes of the people

Rosa Peck was one of the first settlers in Madison. She and her husband ran an inn near the capitol.

Before territories could really run their own governments, they needed time. They needed to have more people to move in and to build more permanent settlements. New settlers also needed time to learn about the needs of the area and "grow into" being a state. But as more and more settlers moved into Wisconsin, the people decided that it was time to become a state.

Why Did Wisconsin Want to Become a State?

Why did people in Wisconsin want to become a state? First, it would give them a greater voice in government. They would be able to elect their own governor and a legislature to make and enforce laws for themselves. As citizens of a state, the people of Wisconsin would also be able to send more representatives and 2 U.S. Senators to Congress. Living in a state also meant that people in Wisconsin could help elect a president. So becoming a state meant that people in Wisconsin could govern themselves by electing state officials and taking part in the federal government as well.

Second, becoming a state meant that people in Wisconsin could raise and spend their own money. As a territory, Wisconsin could spend only the money the U.S.

Congress gave it, much like an allowance you might get from your parents. Becoming a state meant that Wisconsin could raise its own money through taxes, which means money paid to the government. By paying taxes, each person had to help pay for the government. As a state, Wisconsin could also spend the money on whatever the people living there thought needed to be done.

Congress also granted new states large amounts of public land that could be used to pay for public education and construction projects, such as roads, canals, or bridges. When Wisconsin became a state, it would gain more control over its finances and its politics.

In the next chapter, you will learn about the most important step to becoming a state: writing a constitution (kon stuh **too** shun). In the United States, a constitution is a written document (**dah** kyu muhnt) that contains the rights and responsibilities people have and describes how their government will work.

Looking Back

Government is all about people working together. In a democracy, people give government the authority (uh **thor** uh tee) to provide services—like police protection, snow removal, and road construction—that individuals could not do by themselves. In a democracy, people also elect representatives to make the laws that we all have to follow. These laws are created to make life as fair as possible and to keep us safe. In a democracy, everyone has a voice in how the government works.

---

finances: Money   **politics:** The way it governed itself   **document:** A piece of paper containing important information   19
authority: The right to do something or to tell other people what to do

Chapter 2

The Wisconsin Constitution

★ ★ ★

WHS Archives, Classified File 3851, *Milwaukee Journal* photo by Richard Bauer

Why do games like checkers have rules that players need to know?

When you sit down to play a board game with your friends, the first thing you must do is to decide on the rules. Often games have the rules printed right in the box. But a group of friends can always change the rules or make up new ones before they begin to play. Once you decide on the rules, everyone must follow them. A similar thing happens in nations and states.

The U.S. government—and every state government—has a set of rules that was written down a long time ago. These sets of rules are called constitutions. Constitutions are very important documents that maintain order and keep things fair.

Long, long ago, a king made up all the rules as he went along. And the rules almost never applied to him at all! He could change the rules whenever he felt like it, and no one could stop him. But in a democracy, everyone must follow the rules written in a constitution. Even the president must obey them.

When Wisconsin became a state in 1848, the people **adopted** (uh **dop** tud) a constitution to write down the "rules of the game" that we have lived with ever since. The Wisconsin Constitution, like most constitutions, does 2 things. First, it defines the basic rights and responsibilities that everyone has. And second, it describes how the state's government will work.

Questions to Think About

Why is a constitution so important? What does a constitution do? What rights does it protect? What responsibilities does it mention? How did the Wisconsin Constitution change? Why was Wisconsin's first constitution rejected?

---

adopted: Formally accepted and put into use

Constitutions Define Basic Rights and Responsibilities

The need to follow rules is an important responsibility for those in a city, state, and country. But along with this responsibility come many important rights. A constitution defines what those rights are so that they cannot be taken away. For example, the U.S. Constitution has a "Bill of Rights," a list of those freedoms that the authors believed to be the most important in the country's democracy.

The Bill of Rights gives every person the right to express his or her ideas and opinions on any subject. Both the U.S. and Wisconsin Constitutions protect this right by promising that **citizens** (**sit** ih zuhnz) cannot be punished for expressing their ideas. In the United States, everyone born in the country is a citizen. Others can become U.S. citizens if they have lived in the United States legally and long enough to apply for citizenship.

WHS Archives, Classified File 876A

The Bill of Rights protects our freedom of the press, and these newsboys from long ago are out to sell newspapers!

All U.S. citizens have freedom of speech, freedom of religion, and freedom of the press. This means that under the "rules of the game," all people can speak freely on any subject, can worship in any way, and can **publish** anything they want. It is against the law to take these rights away.

It is very important to protect the right of people to do certain things. But it is equally important to **ensure** that certain things *cannot* be done *to* people in our

citizens: Members of a particular country   **publish:** To produce and distribute a book, magazine, newspaper, or any other printed material   **ensure:** To make certain that something happens

country and state. The writers of the U.S. and Wisconsin Constitutions worried that, even in a democracy, government might become too powerful. These wise people knew that kings could do whatever they wanted to their people. That's why the writers listed things that the government officials can *never* do.

Ole Paulson, originally from Norway, received this naturalization certificate in 1913 and became a citizen of the United States.

Both the U.S. and Wisconsin Constitutions ensure that police cannot put you in jail for no reason, cannot search your home, and cannot take your property without just cause. Neither our country nor our state

Anti-Vietnam War protestors in Madison were able to speak out against the war during the 1960s and 1970s because the Bill of Rights protected their freedom of speech.

WHS Archives, PH 6241

can prevent you and others from gathering together to protest against or **petition** (peh **tih** shun) the government.

Even in a democracy, it is important to protect individual people against the power of government. You can think of these 2 sets of rights as "freedoms to" and "freedoms from." We have the freedom *to* speak, but we also have the freedom *from* being sent to jail for saying something unpopular.

WHi Image ID 8622, Milwaukee Journal photo

Why is voting in elections an important reponsibility for all citizens?

With these basic rights come some basic responsibilities. Obeying the law is an obvious responsibility for all people. But people also have a responsibility to help *make* the laws. Of course, all 5 million people of Wisconsin could never gather together in one place to make laws together. Instead, we have a representative government where we vote for a group of legislators to make laws for us. And we vote for a governor to enforce the laws. We have the responsibility to choose the

petition: Request action from

best people for these jobs. Adult citizens can also exercise their rights by deciding to run for office to be elected as a legislator.

Plowing snow in Marinette County, about 1920. The government helps keep things moving, as this photo shows.

We also have the responsibility to pay attention to how well the legislators and the governor do their jobs. If the governor does a poor job, adult citizens have the responsibility to elect someone new at the next election. We also have the responsibility to pay taxes. All the things that government does cost money. That money must come from the people in the form of taxes. If we did not pay any taxes, then no one would plow our streets in the winter! No one would make sure that the food we eat is safe. Or that the air we breathe is clean.

Constitutions Describe Government

In addition to defining the basic rights and responsibilities that every person has, constitutions also explain how government is going to work. For example, the U.S. Constitution created the Offices of the U.S. President, Congress, and the Supreme Court. The constitution also explained how the president is elected, how states send representatives to Congress, and how the Court works. We still follow these rules.

The Wisconsin Constitution does exactly the same thing. The constitution also describes how to make laws. The constitution describes how the people select legislators and how the government enforces laws, collects taxes, and provides services.

But what if people disagree with laws or break these laws? The constitution also establishes a supreme court to settle these differences peacefully. These functions of government are known as the 3 branches:

the 📜 **legislative** (lej uh **slay** tiv)

the 🦅 **executive** (eg **zek** yuh tiv)

the ⚖️ **judicial** (joo **dish** uhl).

You'll learn more about each in the next chapter.

Journal of the Convention to form a Constitution for the State of Wisconsin, WHS Library

CONSTITUTION

OF THE

STATE OF WISCONSIN.

ADOPTED IN CONVENTION AT MADISON,

February 1st, A. D. 1848.

———

PREAMBLE.

We, the people of Wisconsin, grateful to Almighty God for our freedom, in order to secure its blessings, form a more perfect government, insure domestic tranquility, and promote the general welfare, do establish this Constitution.

ARTICLE I.

DECLARATION OF RIGHTS.

Section 1. All men are born equally free and independent, and have certain inherent rights: among these are life, liberty, and the pursuit of happiness. To secure these rights governments are instituted among men, deriving their just powers from the consent of the governed.

Sec. 2. There shall be neither slavery nor involuntary servitude in this state, otherwise than for the punishment of crime, whereof the party shall have been duly convicted.

Sec. 3. Every person may freely speak, write, and publish his sentiments on all subjects, being responsible for the abuse of that right, and no laws shall be passed to restrain or abridge the liberty of speech or of the press. In all criminal prosecutions or indictments for libel, the truth may be given in evidence, and if it shall appear to the jury that the matter charged as libellous be true, and was published with good motives and for justifiable ends, the party shall be acquitted; and the jury shall have the right to determine the law and the fact.

Sec. 4. The right of the people peaceably to assemble to consult for the common good, to petition the government or any department thereof, shall never be abridged.

Sec. 5. The right of trial by jury shall remain inviolate; and shall
76

The first page of the Wisconsin Constitution, 1848

Constitutions Can Change . . . Sometimes

What happens when you and your friends are playing a game and decide that you need to change the rules? How do you decide what changes to make?

The writers of the Wisconsin Constitution faced a similar question. They recognized that, in the future, people might want to change the constitution. But since the constitution contains the most important rules, the people who wrote the constitution thought that it should be hard to change.

The writers of our Wisconsin Constitution also wanted changing the constitution to be democratic. They feared that a small group of people might gain control of the government and rewrite the constitution to suit only themselves. Perhaps they would even take away some of the other people's most important rights!

Wisconsin's Constitution *can* be **amended**, or changed. But it is a long process that requires lawmakers to think very carefully about the changes. First, some legislators must write out the change that's wanted.

Women did not always have the right to vote in Wisconsin. Many women, like Mrs. McCullough in this 1912 photograph, were active in demanding that right.

27

Then members of the legislature must vote to approve a change to the constitution. The legislature must do this twice in 2 different **sessions**. Second, the voters must approve the amendment to the constitution in an election, voting yes or no on the proposed changes.

Between 1848 and 2004, the people living in Wisconsin made 139 changes to the state constitution. For example, in 1967 voters approved an amendment that gave governors 4-year terms instead of 2-year terms of office.

The Need for Consensus

Let's return to the example of playing a board game. When you are making the rules to your game, does everyone have to agree? What happens if almost everyone wants a rule to change, but one person doesn't? Do you vote on the rule, or do you **compromise** (**com** pruh mize)?

Some decisions are too important to decide by simply voting. In these cases a **consensus** (cun **sen** sus) must be reached. Consensus

Sorry! is a popular board game with rules that are easy to follow.

means that everyone meeting consents or agrees. Nobody gets everything he or she wants, but everyone is satisfied with the final decision. Reaching a consensus usually requires a great deal of discussion and some compromise to make everyone happy.

sessions: Times when the legislature meets **compromise:** To agree to accept something that is not exactly what you wanted

This painting, which hangs in the Wisconsin Supreme Court in the capitol, shows the signing of the U.S. Constitution.

The U.S. Constitution is a good example of compromise. **Delegates** (**deh** luh guts) from the states gathered in Philadelphia in 1787 to write the constitution. Many of these delegates had different ideas about how the federal government should work. Delegates from small states thought that each state should be represented equally in Congress. Those from larger states thought that equal representation was unfair. They felt that states with more people should have more representatives.

In the end, the delegates reached a compromise. They decided that the U.S. Congress should consist of 2 houses. Each house represented one of these 2 major ideas. In the **Senate** (**sen** it), states are represented equally. In the **House of Representatives**, states are represented based on the number of people living there.

delegates: People selected to represent other people at a meeting

29

Adopting a constitution for Wisconsin was much harder. In fact, Wisconsin had to do it *twice!* Why do you think that happened? In 1846, delegates from around the state gathered in Madison to write a constitution, but they could not reach a consensus. Most voters rejected the constitution. So, in 1847, a second group of delegates had to write another constitution.

The Story of Wisconsin's Constitution

By April 1846, Wisconsin had been a U.S. territory for 10 years. Then Wisconsin voters decided that they wanted to become a state. The U.S. Congress required that each territory had to write a constitution before it could become a state. That fall, Wisconsin voters elected a total of 124 delegates to meet in Madison to write a constitution.

For months, these delegates discussed how the state government should work. They also discussed what rights and responsibilities the people should have. They decided on some parts of the constitution very quickly. For example, delegates created a legislature with 2 houses—the **assembly** (uh **sem** blee) and the senate—modeled on the U.S. Congress. Delegates agreed on an office of the governor that was very similar to governors' offices in other states.

Some questions were harder to decide. Should court judges be elected by the people or be appointed by the governor? The U.S. Constitution called for federal judges to be appointed by the president, and many states followed this example. Some states let the people choose judges through elections. Many Wisconsin delegates thought that electing judges seemed much more democratic. After much

debate (duh **bate**), the delegates decided that the people of Wisconsin should elect their judges.

Another difficult decision involved who would be able to vote. Today all citizens can vote. In 1846, only male citizens were allowed to vote. Some delegates wanted to give immigrants the right to vote, as long as the immigrants

The mural "Wisconsin" presents a story about the past, present, and future of the state of Wisconsin. It hangs in the Assembly Chamber in the capitol.

intended to become citizens. Some other delegates thought it was not fair to let non-citizens vote. Finally, the delegates decided to allow non-citizens to vote only if they had lived in Wisconsin for at least one year.

But the **convention** (cun **ven** chun) did not allow the right to vote to any people other than males who were born in the United States and males who had become legal citizens of the country. Nobody seriously suggested that women be given the right to vote. That's because in the 1840s women were not allowed to vote *anywhere*

debate: A discussion between sides with different views **convention:** A large gathering of people who share the same interests

in the United States! And during the 1840s, American Indian men were members of their sovereign American Indian nations, but they were not allowed to be citizens of the United States.

Nor were African American men given the right to vote. In 1846, hundreds of thousands of African Americans were still slaves in the southern United States. Some free African Americans lived in the north. But these African Americans were seldom allowed to vote, even though they were not slaves and had been born in the United States. At the same time the Wisconsin voters decided on the constitution, they would decide if African Americans could vote.

Edward Ryan was a strong voice in Wisconsin's 1846 Constitutional Convention.
WHi (X3) 10920

The greatest arguments surrounded the part of the constitution that allowed married women the right to own their own property. In this case, property meant land. In the United States at this time, a woman's property became her husband's after marriage. Any property she might gain after marriage became her husband's, too. Some delegates thought this was wrong. These delegates wanted the constitution to guarantee women the right to keep their own property. Other delegates were alarmed by the proposal. They believed men should always have more control.

Racine delegates Edward Ryan and Marshall Strong spoke out. They believed that women should not be able to vote or own property. But David Noggle of Beloit finally

Women worked hard in their homes for many years but still were not able to vote in Wisconsin until 1919.

pointed out that men already trusted their wives with the care of their homes and their children. It was silly to think that women could not own their own property!

At this point, the consensus broke down. Angry, Marshall Strong left the convention. He promised that he would work to defeat the constitution when the people of Wisconsin voted on it. And he did. Between December 16, 1846, and April 6, 1847, when Wisconsin citizens voted on the constitution, a great debate raged over the document.

Strong wanted voters to reject the constitution because it gave women property rights. Other people in Wisconsin did not like the constitution for other reasons. Some did not like the constitution because it did not give African American men the right to vote. A newspaper in Waukesha County, the *American Freeman*, expressed this viewpoint. The newspaper demanded that voters reject the constitution because it did not provide equal rights. In the end, more people voted to **reject** the constitution than voted for it. Sadly, even more people voted to deny Wisconsin African American males the right to vote.

Why didn't Marshall Strong like the 1846 Constitution?

WHS Archives, Name File

reject: To turn down or vote against something

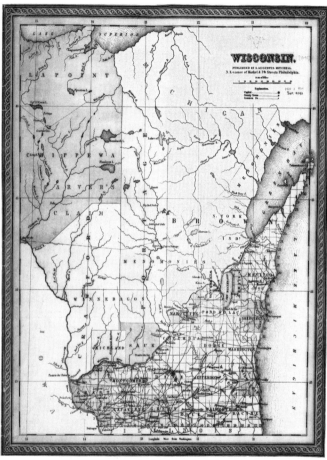

Map of Wisconsin, 1848. The counties show that most of the settlement was in the southwestern and southeastern part of the state.

Voters had rejected the constitution. What would happen next? At this point, Governor Henry Dodge took action. He called a special session of the legislature in October to fix the situation. Within 10 days, the legislature passed a law calling for a new convention to be composed of just 69 delegates to meet on December 15. The smaller number of delegates made the convention easier to manage and made it easier for a consensus to be reached.

The delegates had to rewrite the constitution. It took only 7 weeks to finish the job. The new constitution left out the ideas that had caused so much debate. The writers dropped providing property rights for married women. And they offered the people a *chance* to vote on the African American vote sometime in the future.

These changes allowed the convention and the people to reach a consensus on the new constitution. In March 1848, people voted on the constitution. This time, ¾ of the voters approved the new constitution. The final step in the statehood process occurred on May 29, 1848, when President James K. Polk admitted the state of Wisconsin into the **union**, or the federal government.

James K. Polk was President of the United States when Wisconsin became a state.

WHS Archives, Name File

Looking Back

In a democracy, everybody has the responsibility to follow the rules and obey the law. But people also have the responsibility to help *make* those laws. People elect a legislature, a governor, and a court that will create and enforce good laws. Along with these responsibilities come many rights. In a democracy, everyone has the right to speak and worship freely. Everyone also has the right to be protected from unfair action by the government.

The first attempt to create a Wisconsin Constitution in 1846 failed because voters rejected it. To achieve consensus, the rewritten constitution left out ideas that caused too much debate. One of these ideas was giving women property rights. Voters accepted the new Wisconsin Constitution. It describes the basic rights and responsibilities of Wisconsin citizens. It also tells people how the state government works. Although the constitution has been changed many times, it still provides the "rules of the game" for Wisconsin.

union: Another name for the federal government

Chapter 3
State Government and Tribal Government

★ ★ ★

Do you ever go to baseball games? When the team is in the outfield, different players play different positions and work together to win. Similarly, many people do different jobs in Wisconsin's government, but they all cooperate to make the state work.

In Chapter 2, you learned how the people of Wisconsin adopted a constitution in 1848 in order to become a state. The constitution showed how state government should work. The writers of the Wisconsin Constitution followed the pattern of the U.S. Constitution.

WHi Image ID 7138

Uniforms have changed since this 1900 baseball game in Whitewater, but you can still recognize the batter, catcher, and umpire.

State government has 3 different branches, just like the U.S. government. Each branch of government has a really big name, does many jobs, and has its own responsibilities.

First, the **legislative** (**lej** uh slay tiv) branch is the law-making branch of government. It creates laws for everyone in the state to follow.

Next is the **executive** (eg **zek** yu tiv) branch. The executive is the governor, who is the head of the state. He or she **executes** (**eg** zeh kyoots), or puts into action and enforces, all the laws of the state.

Finally, the judges and the courts of law make up the **judicial** (ju **dish** uhl) branch. The judicial branch has the responsibility to solve the problems that come up as people disagree on what the law means. Their solutions are called **judgments**.

In this chapter, you'll find out what each branch actually *does* in Wisconsin's state government. And you'll see why these 3 branches keep democracy strong.

You'll also learn about how Indian Nations set up their own tribal governments on state reservations. These governments help tribal members living on and off the reservation.

Questions to Think About

What does each of the 3 branches of state government do? How does each branch improve democracy in Wisconsin? How are tribal governments both similar to and different from state government?

Key to 3 Branches of State Government

Legislative

Executive

Judicial

37

The 3 Branches of State Government

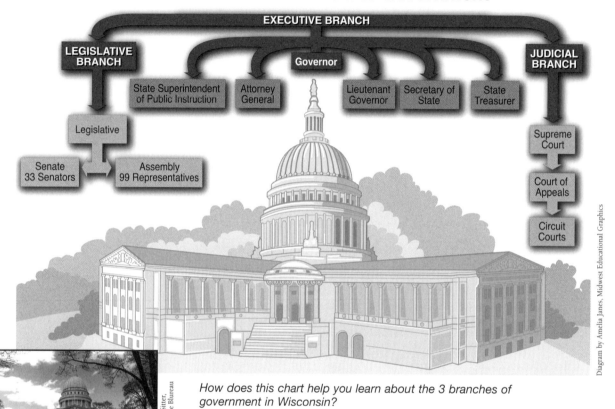

Diagram by Amelia Janes, Midwest Educational Graphics

How does this chart help you learn about the 3 branches of government in Wisconsin?

All 3 branches of state government make their home in the state capitol in Madison.

Photo by Kathleen Sitter, Legislative Reference Bureau

The Legislative Branch

The legislative branch contains 2 different law-making groups. They make up the 2 houses of state government. Wisconsin citizens elect people to each house. One house is known as the senate. Those elected to serve in the senate are called senators. The other house is the assembly. Those elected to the assembly are called representatives. Both senators and representatives serve the interests of the people who elected them.

This photo shows the area of the supreme court where the judges sit. The painting is on page 29.

The governor's office is one of the most beautiful rooms in the capitol.

This photo shows the room at the capitol where senators meet.

The 1947–48 State Assembly looks very busy. The representatives have plenty of books to study!

The senate and the assembly are not the same size. Here comes some math! An important difference between the 2 houses is that the senate is smaller than the assembly. In fact, there are 3 times as many representatives in Wisconsin as there are senators. The state is divided into 33 senate districts, as you can see on the map on page 40. The people of each district elect a senator to represent them in the senate. That makes 33 senators total.

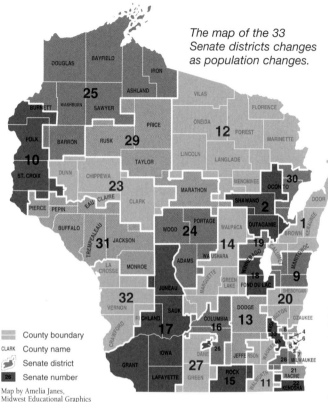

The map of the 33 Senate districts changes as population changes.

County boundary
CLARK County name
Senate district
26 Senate number

Map by Amelia Janes,
Midwest Educational Graphics

Remember that the assembly is larger. If there are 3 assembly districts in every senate district, how many assembly districts are there?

Each of the 33 senate districts is divided into 3 assembly districts. This makes a total of 99 assembly districts. And each of the 99 assembly districts elects a representative to the assembly. That means that there are 33 senators and 99 representatives in all.

Why does the legislature have 2 houses instead of one? In part, the Wisconsin legislature is organized like the U.S. Congress, which has a House of Representatives and a Senate. Almost all other states copied this organization.

Members of both houses can write and **propose** (pruh poze) new laws. These proposed laws are called **bills** . Each bill is debated and eventually approved or turned down. When writing and talking about bills, representatives and senators must think about the needs of the people they

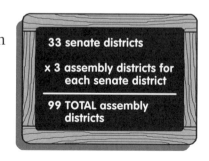

33 senate districts

x 3 assembly districts for each senate district

99 TOTAL assembly districts

School students, their teachers, and other adults are watching the 1947–48 legislators in the assembly do their work.

represent in their districts. The representatives and senators must also think about the needs of the people throughout the state.

In Wisconsin, having 2 houses helps keep the legislature democratic, that is, truly representing the needs of the people. First, each house has to pass a bill in order for it to become a law. This gives people around the state an opportunity to write to their legislators to tell them how they feel about the bill. Because leaders in the assembly and the senate debate the same bill, it gets a great deal of attention.

Why is twice the attention good? Debating a bill takes many hours. All of this time spent talking about and listening to both sides of a debate helps legislators think through the bill. The debating prevents bad ideas in a bill from being made into a law too quickly. Both houses have a chance to make changes to the bill or catch mistakes. If there were only one house, it would be easier for a bad idea to become a law.

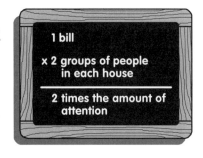

1 bill

x 2 groups of people in each house

2 times the amount of attention

Second, having 2 houses in the legislature keeps senators and representatives in touch with their people. Remember that there are 99 assembly districts, and all are smaller than senate districts. So each representative in the assembly represents about 54,000 people, while a senator represents about 163,000 people. This means that it is easier for each representative to know the issues that matter to the people in that district.

Governor Tommy Thompson signs bills on April 27, 1990. One of these became the law for statewide recycling.

Because senate districts are larger, senators have to represent the views of more people in a larger part of the state. It's like at school where teachers know lots about the students in their classrooms. But the principal may know a little about every student in every classroom in the school.

For example, the 29th Wisconsin Senate District includes much of 4 counties—Marathon, Taylor, Price, and Rusk—as well as the cities of Wausau (**wah** saw) and Mosinee (**mo** zih nee). The senator from the 29th Wisconsin Senate District represents a large area that includes farms, small towns, and cities. He or she must support laws that are in the best interests of *all* these people.

The 29th Wisconsin Senate District is divided into 3 assembly districts (the 85th, 86th, and 87th). The 87th Wisconsin Assembly District contains almost entirely

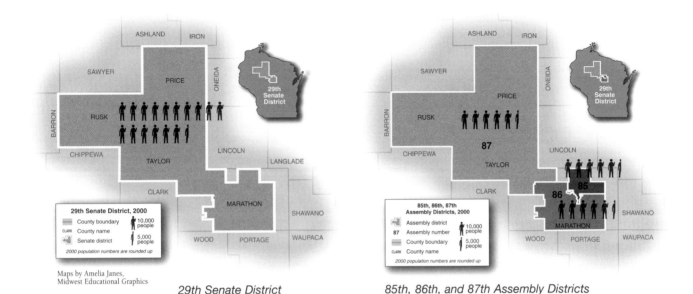

29th Senate District

85th, 86th, and 87th Assembly Districts

Maps by Amelia Janes,
Midwest Educational Graphics

rural (**rur** uhl) farm areas, so voters there are more likely to ask their representatives to pay special attention to issues that affect farmers.

The 85th Wisconsin Assembly District is smaller and includes the city of Wausau. Voters there are more likely to ask their representative to pay more attention to issues affecting small cities. The 86th Wisconsin Assembly District is more like the 87th, but it does have the city of Mosinee. Its representative will have to pay attention to the needs of farmers *and* those living in small cities. Having 2 houses makes it easier for all these points of view to be represented.

Representatives to the assembly serve 2-year terms, and senators serve 4-year terms. Are you keeping score?

rural: Having to do with the countryside or farming

43

Senators and representatives have to think about the opinions of the many different people who live in their districts. Both of these locations are in the 29th Wisconsin Senate District. How might the concerns of business people in downtown Wausau be different from those of people living outside of the city?

The number of representatives and senators has changed since Wisconsin became a state. The number of legislators increased as new parts of the state were settled, and each of these areas sent representatives to Madison. Since 1973, the system we have had includes 33 senators and 99 representatives.

Now each senate district can be evenly divided into 3 assembly districts. It helps when math problems come out evenly, especially when that math involves people!

You've used vocabulary skills and math skills. Now here come the map skills! Both senate and assembly districts are all *supposed* to be equal in **population** (pop yu **lay** shun). Keeping the districts equal helps keep representation fair. Each person should have an equal voice. So each representative and senator should represent the same number of people.

population: The total number of people living in a specific place

But how does the legislature keep the districts equal? This story is about to get more complicated. Over time, the number of people in some districts grows faster than in other districts. And some districts actually lose population. When these changes happen, districts become unequal. Changes must be made.

Every 10 years the U.S. government conducts a **census** (**sen** sus). That's when the government hires people to count *everybody* who lives in the United States. After the census, we know how unequal the districts have become. This means that every 10 years the legislature must redraw the map of the districts to keep them equal!

If you do not redistrict every 10 years, these differences between districts get larger and larger. For many years, the legislature did not redistrict after every census. By the 1950s and 1960s, redrawing districts became more difficult. During those years, many people moved out of cities like Milwaukee into nearby **suburban** (suh **bur** bun) areas like Waukesha. Like other suburbs, Waukesha grew very quickly. At the same time, people were moving away from rural areas like Douglas County. Douglas County saw its population shrink.

As people moved from Milwaukee to suburban areas in the 33rd Wisconsin Senate District (made up of Waukesha and Jefferson Counties), this district had 3 times as many people living there as the 25th Wisconsin Senate District (made up of Ashland, Bayfield, and Douglas Counties). Only one senator represented each of these districts, even though many more people lived in the 33rd District than in the 25th District. This means that people in the 33rd District had less of a voice in the senate than those living in the 25th District. That's not fair!

suburban: Areas on the outskirts of cities with more homes than businesses

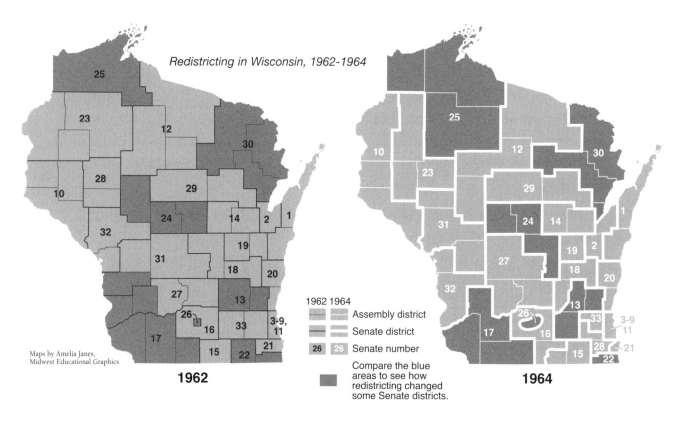

Redistricting in Wisconsin, 1962-1964

Maps by Amelia Janes,
Midwest Educational Graphics

1962 1964	
Assembly district	
Senate district	
26 26	Senate number

Compare the blue areas to see how redistricting changed some Senate districts.

1962

1964

Things were even worse in the assembly. One Waukesha Assembly District had more than 4 times the population of a Douglas County Assembly District! After legislators were unable to solve the problem, the state supreme court redrew the district maps to make them fairer. Population has continued to change since then. Redistricting is still a major problem every 10 years. Each community needs to have an equal voice in the legislature!

46

The Executive Branch

The governor heads the executive branch of Wisconsin's government. The governor represents *all* the people in the state. Just like state senators, the governor is elected every 4 years. The governor enforces the laws passed by the legislature and oversees the daily management of the state. The governor cannot do everything, of course. So he or she **appoints** people to manage the major state departments, like the Department of Health and Family Services or the Department of Natural Resources. Some of the governor's most important jobs are to propose a state budget and suggest new laws to the legislature.

The Wisconsin Constitution created several other executive officers to assist the governor and do some of the most important jobs in the state. The men who wrote the constitution thought these jobs were so important that the voters should elect these leaders rather than allow the governor to appoint them.

★ First, the lieutenant governor is the state's "second-in-command" and carries out the duties of the governor if the governor is out of state. If the governor dies or leaves office, the lieutenant governor becomes governor.

WHS Archives, Name File

When Gaylord Nelson was governor of Wisconsin, he visited Washington, D.C. He then became famous as the U.S. Senator who started Earth Day.

appoints: Chooses people for a particular job or duty

In 1939, many rural Wisconsin students attended one-room schools like this one in the western part of the state.

The superintendent of public instruction runs all the state public schools, from one-room schools to large schools in cities, such as this one in Appleton.

★ The secretary of state has duties, such as writing down the official acts of the governor and legislature and attaching the Great Seal of the State of Wisconsin to state papers.

★ The attorney general represents the state in court, provides legal advice to the governor and other state officials, and enforces state laws.

★ The state treasurer receives and pays out money for the state.

★ The superintendent of public instruction leads the state public school system in making decisions—from kindergarten to high school. The superintendent also issues licenses to teachers and principals and inspects schools.

The state seal, created in 1881, shows many things that are important parts of Wisconsin's history.

The Judicial Branch

Judges make up the judicial branch of government. You found out how and why state and local governments make laws that people must obey. Now you're going to learn about what happens when people break those laws. Watch out for more new words!

Judges are responsible for deciding on disagreements (dis uh **gree** muntz) between people over state law. They also are in charge of **trying** a person accused of breaking a law. Trying or bringing that person to judgment in a court of law is known as a **trial** (**try** uhl).

SUPREME COURT
Chief Justice

COURT OF APPEALS
Chief Judge

The levels of courts in Wisconsin's judicial branch

MUNICIPAL COURTS

CIRCUIT COURTS
Chief Judge
(10 Administrative Districts)

Graphic by Amelia Janes,
Midwest Educational Graphics

Remember the legislative branch, with 2 houses of government at the state level? The judicial branch is different: it has courts at 3 levels. At the lowest level is the **circuit** (**sur** cut) court. At the next level is the **court of appeals**, and at the top is the **supreme court**.

When someone is accused of breaking a state law, he or she is tried in a circuit court at the county level, in which a judge determines the facts and decides how the law should deal with the case.

trying: Bringing to trial or to court

In Wisconsin, the constitution guarantees every person the right to have a trial by jury. Every person also has the right to be defended in court by a lawyer. In court, there are always 2 sides represented. The lawyer for the defense defends the **defendant**, the person accused of breaking the law. The district attorney represents the state in an individual case. The state presents **charges** against the defendant and **evidence** (**ev** uh duhnts).

A lawyer argues his case in front of the 1947 Wisconsin Supreme Court.

WHY IS IT CALLED "CIRCUIT" COURT?

You might think that "circuit court" is an odd name, but it comes from the way judges originally ran their courts. When Wisconsin became a state, there were many small communities that needed a judge. But few communities were large enough to need one judge all to themselves. So a judge traveled in a **circuit**, or a circular path, from community to community in a certain area. The judge had a regular schedule to conduct trial cases. The judge's journey from place to place was called a circuit, because the judge made a circle around the area. Now most counties have a circuit court judge who stays in one place all the time. The practice has changed, but the name remains.

charges: Blaming someone for a particular thing **evidence:** Information and facts that help prove something or make you believe something is true

In court, the district attorney acts as the **prosecutor** (**pross** uh kyoo tur). The prosecutor presents these charges and evidence to the judge and a jury. A jury hears the evidence from both sides. The jury then meets to decide whether the defendant is guilty or innocent. But that is not always where the story ends.

The prosecutor or the defendant may not be satisfied with the result of a circuit court trial. Either side may then **appeal** the decision to the next highest level, the Wisconsin Court of Appeals. The court of appeals reviews the case and decides whether or not the trial was fair.

The court of appeals decision may *still* seem unfair to the prosecutor or the defendant. Then there is one more appeal to be made. This step is to take the case to the Wisconsin Supreme Court, the top level and most important part of the judicial branch.

prosecutor: A lawyer who represents the government in criminal cases **appeal:** To ask that a decision made by a court of law be changed

The 2004 Wisconsin Supreme Court in the courtroom you saw on page 39

Not many cases go all the way up to the supreme court. The supreme court consists of 7 justices who are elected to 10-year terms. The justice who has been on the court the longest is the chief justice. The supreme court only hears appeals from lower courts' decisions and decides if a person has had a fair trial. The court also settles disputes over the constitution. If 2 people have different views of a part of the constitution, the supreme court decides which view is right.

Checks and Balances

Like the writers of the U.S. Constitution, those who wrote the Wisconsin Constitution had good reasons to keep government organized. They called for a government divided into 3 branches, each with its own responsibilities. This kind of organization was formed to keep any one part of state government from becoming too powerful. Even though Wisconsin is a democracy, the men who wrote the state constitution wanted to make sure that the governor did not exercise too much power over people's lives.

Of course, the writers of the Wisconsin Constitution also did not want the legislature to have too much authority. Having 3 branches makes sure that each branch watches the others. These "checks and balances" keep all 3 responsible to the citizens of Wisconsin.

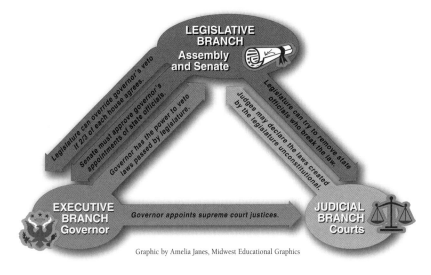

Graphic by Amelia Janes, Midwest Educational Graphics

Can you follow the checks and balances in our government?

How does the system of "checks and balances" actually work? Even though each branch has its own responsibilities, each branch is given a little power over the other 2. For example, the legislature passes laws, but the governor has the power to **veto** (**vee** toh), or reject a law. The legislature can only **override** this veto if ⅔ of each house agrees that the governor is wrong.

Remember that the legislature also has some control over the governor. The governor appoints many state officials. But here's the "check": the senate must approve those appointments. Another check is the supreme court, which has power over the legislature *and* the governor.

override: Cancel

TRIBAL GOVERNMENTS

Because the Native peoples of Wisconsin are sovereign, they have their own governments that protect the rights of tribal citizens and provide services for them. Every Indian Nation has its own constitution that creates a tribal government. There are 11 federally recognized Indian reservations or tribal lands in Wisconsin. On reservations tribal governments are sovereign.

Photo by Joseph W. Jackson III, Wisconsin State Journal

These tribal governments are similar to Wisconsin's. But they also show the way Native people have always governed themselves. The Ho-Chunk government, for example, includes 4 branches of tribal government: the executive, legislative, judicial, and also a General Council. The General Council meets at least once a year and includes all members of the tribe. The governments of other tribes are also organized into different branches.

Volunteers from some of the state's 11 recognized American Indian nations carry feather flags into the assembly chambers before the first State of the Tribes address.

Tribal governments work very much like other governments. Tribal members elect representatives to a tribal legislature. The tribal legislature passes laws that affect tribal members. Each tribe has an executive who leads and enforces those laws. The executive branch is responsible for providing health care, education, and other services for all tribal members. The tribal court system decides disagreements between tribal members. But not every tribe has a court system.

Tribal governments also preserve the Nation's history and culture. Most Indian Nations have a tribal historian who keeps the traditional histories of the Nation and teaches them to members' children. Preserving culture and language is a very important part of tribal sovereignty and government.

The supreme court can declare laws or executive actions by the governor **unconstitutional** (uhn con stih **too** shun uhl), or against the rules described in the constitution. This judicial power means that the supreme court has the final say over whether the legislature and the governor are following "the rules of the game."

But to balance these checks, the governor and the legislature have some power over the court as well. The governor appoints justices to the supreme court when there are **vacancies** (**va** cuhn sees), or when one of the justices retires or dies. And the legislature has the power to try and remove any state official—including supreme court justices—who breaks the law.

Looking Back

Most of the state is governed by government divided into 3 branches—the legislative, the executive, and the judicial. The people elect representatives and senators to the legislature to make laws and elect a governor to carry them out. The people also elect 7 supreme court justices to resolve disagreements over laws and the constitution. Dividing government keeps all 3 branches responsible to the people.

Each of the 11 Indian Nations has its own lands. And each has its own constitution. Tribal governments create laws that protect their rights and sovereignty. These governments also provide important services to the people, like health care, education, and preservation of their language and culture.

All citizens of Wisconsin are under either state or tribal government. They can expect that the government's laws and lawmakers will operate fairly to protect everyone. If not, citizens can elect new people to represent them.

vacancies: Not occupied, as a job that is available

Chapter 4

Government Working for the People

★ ★ ★

Think about the way your school works. The principal is in charge of the school and makes many of the rules you have to follow. But one person cannot do everything. Your principal probably has others to help. Perhaps your school has a vice principal. Certainly there are secretaries to answer the telephone and help students and teachers. Your principal hires teachers to teach students. And the principal has custodians to help take care of the school and keep it clean.

Immigrant Polish farmers are learning the latest scientific information from University of Wisconsin–Extension agricultural experts. The UW–Extension program brought the University to people around the state to help them work and live better.

In Chapter 3, you learned how the governor heads the executive branch of state government. The governor is responsible for enforcing state laws and generally running the state. Just as your principal needs many others to make your school run smoothly, Wisconsin's governor needs many people to help run the state, too. They do the hard work to make the state's many **agencies** (**a** juhn seez) serve the people of Wisconsin.

Since 1848, the executive branch of government has changed a great deal. Its main responsibilities—keeping people safe and trying to make things fair—have remained the same. But the services provided by the government have really grown as our state has grown.

Wisconsin has become a state of more than 5 million people and a land of agriculture, **manufacturing** (man yuh **fak** chur ring), and business. The ways in which we must all work together to keep people safe has increased. So have the ways in which a democratic government can make life fairer for all people in Wisconsin. In this chapter, you will learn about the many things that the executive branch can do to make a better life for everyone.

Questions to Think About

What are some of the most important things that the government does to help people in the state? What people help carry out the governor's many responsibilities? What are the kinds of things that our state government does to protect its citizens?

agencies: Offices that provide services to the public   **manufacturing:** Making something, often with machines

57

Teaching the People

In a democracy, everyone needs to have an education. In school, students learn the rights and responsibilities that are key to a democracy like ours. They learn to think about and debate different points of view. When the students become adults, they use the skills they learned in school to help them to choose good leaders for different levels of government.

Students and teachers in a Milwaukee school, 1909

But getting an education costs a great deal of money. It would be unfair for some people to have an education and not others. That's why, since 1848, the state of Wisconsin has provided public education for its people.

The state constitution created the Office of Superintendent of Public Instruction and required the legislature to create schools that anyone aged 4–20 could attend *for free*. To ensure these schools provided a good education, the superintendent originally had 2 main jobs.

First, the superintendent gave local schools money. Schools in Wisconsin received money through the sale of public land. This money, along with money raised locally through taxes, was used to construct schoolhouses, hire teachers, and provide supplies.

Second, the superintendent inspected schools. He was required to visit schools in every county, recommend textbooks, and tell the schools what subjects to teach.

Beginning in 1868, the superintendent took on a third responsibility: **licensing** (**ly** suhn sing) teachers. By requiring every teacher to be trained and have a license, the Wisconsin Department of Public Instruction (DPI) can make sure that every school has well-trained teachers.

At first, Wisconsin public schools offered only a basic, or "elementary," education. Classes included subjects like reading, writing, math, and history. In 1875, the state began offering more education to more people by opening public high schools. High schools offered classes in more complicated subjects, like geometry, algebra, and science.

THE GOOD CITIZEN
Does Not
Play Ball in the Street
Uncover Sewers or Coal Chutes
Break Glass in the Street
Use a Bean-Shooter
Tease Animals

Citizenship and government have always been important subjects for students to study. What details tell you that this poster is not new?

How did Wisconsin teachers learn to teach? At first, many of the teachers who worked in public schools received their education from colleges in other states. And some teachers had very little education.

As the number of students increased, the state saw the need to provide better training for its teachers. The state created "Normal Schools" to train teachers. The first was opened in Platteville in 1866 and was followed by others: Whitewater

licensing: Giving official permission to do something

STATE OF WISCONSIN
DEPARTMENT OF PUBLIC INSTRUCTION
MADISON

4071

TWO YEAR LICENSE

This Is to Certify That __Doris Anne Bednarek__

is a graduate of __Wisconsin State College @ Oshkosh__

and is hereby licensed to teach __Grades one to three inclusive__

in any public elem school in this state until __July 1, 1956__

In Witness Whereof, I have hereunto affixed my signature and official seal, at the City of Madison, this

__6th__ day of __August__ 195_4_

State Superintendent

No. 1654

Elementary school teaching license

The Normal School in River Falls, 1872–1882

(1868), Oshkosh (1871), and River Falls (1873). Over the next 40 years, additional Normal Schools were opened in Stevens Point, Milwaukee, La Crosse, Superior, and Eau Claire.

More and more Wisconsin young people finished high schools and wanted a college education. So these teachers' colleges began offering a full course of study and awarding college degrees in many fields. They became **universities** (yoo nuh **vur** suh teez). Today all of these universities, such as UW–Stevens Point and UW–Whitewater, are part of the University of Wisconsin **system** (**sis** tum). Students in Wisconsin could afford to attend these public universities and receive a good college education near their homes.

During the 20th century, the state continued its role in education. Today, the Wisconsin Department of Public Instruction still licenses teachers and provides training and resources to teachers and libraries. The DPI also sets standards for graduation and gives tests to students to make sure that schools are doing a good job.

universities: Schools for higher education after high school. Universities are organized into colleges for different fields of study.   **system:** A group of things that work in an organized way

One of the DPI's most important responsibilities is to distribute state funds to local schools. Since 1927, Wisconsin has tried to equalize school districts, or provide more money to poorer school districts and less to wealthy school districts. This funding makes education fairer by assuring every child in the state a good education. Without government, only the richest people could go to school.

North Hall was the first building on the University of Wisconsin campus in Madison.

The kind of democracy our citizens value would not be possible without good education. And the early leaders of Wisconsin recognized the need to provide the highest possible education to the people. In 1848, the legislature established the University of Wisconsin in Madison. The university provided a government-supported education to anyone who wanted it.

The construction of the buildings began the following year. There were 20 students

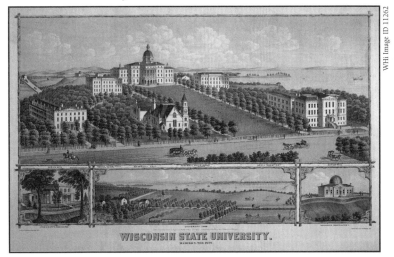

This 1879 print of the University of Wisconsin is known as a bird's-eye view. The campus and the University of Wisconsin system have grown a lot since then!

enrolled in the first classes. In 1854 the University of Wisconsin awarded degrees to its first class, which had only 2 graduates! Many years later, the University of Wisconsin–Madison became the main campus (and the largest) in the University of Wisconsin system.

The people of Wisconsin recognized early on that the University of Wisconsin could do more than just provide education to its students. The university could provide education to *all* the people, wherever they lived in the state. In 1893, the University of Wisconsin–Extension was created to "extend" classes. Then every person who was interested could learn more about *any* subject.

Through the Extension program, professors traveled to towns and cities to deliver lectures. And experts from the College of Agriculture provided advice for farmers.

The University of Wisconsin-Extension traveled all over the state to give advice to farmers to help them improve their crops.

Today, the University of Wisconsin-Extension continues to provide education and training to people around the state. The most important job of the Extension is to work with the Educational Communications Board (ECB). The ECB produces Wisconsin Public Radio and Wisconsin Public Television. These broadcasts bring education to every corner of the state and right into people's homes and into classrooms. All of these programs are free to those who live in Wisconsin.

THE FIRST RADIO STATION IN THE NATION

We take radio stations for granted today. But in the early 1900s, they were new and exciting. Two University of Wisconsin professors, Edward Bennett and Earle M. Terry, began broadcasting wireless messages. In 1915, the university received a license to broadcast from the federal government with the call letters 9XM. Radio station 9XM began broadcasting daily weather reports and even began broadcasting music. In 1922, the station's call letters were changed to WHA. Today, the station is the oldest radio station in the United States.

WHS Archives, PH 2612

Many students in the state, like these fourth-grade students, listened to educational radio programs on WHA. Do you do something similar in your classroom?

Today, the University of Wisconsin at Madison is part of the statewide University of Wisconsin system. The system was created in 1971. That's when the University of Wisconsin and the University Extension joined with the smaller state universities around the state. Today, the University of Wisconsin System consists of 13 4-year universities and 13 2-year colleges. Without everyone working together through government, these educational opportunities would not be possible.

John Commons
WHS Archives, Name File

WORKING FOR WORKING PEOPLE: JOHN R. COMMONS

University of Wisconsin Professor John R. Commons helped build 2 of Wisconsin's most important programs to help working people. In the early 1900s, Commons studied problems facing **industrial** (in **duhss** tree uhl) workers in the United States. He discovered that they were at great risk of getting hurt and losing their jobs. He helped the state develop programs to protect both injured workers and those who had lost their jobs. Wisconsin became a national leader in taking care of its citizens.

WHi Image ID 9029

Zinc mining was a dangerous industrial job.

Today, the University of Wisconsin system has locations all over the state.

Institutions in the University of Wisconsin System

- UW-Superior
- UW-Barron County
- UW-Marinette
- UW-Stout
- UW-Marathon County
- UW-River Falls
- UW-Eau Claire
- UW-Marshfield/Wood County
- UW-Stevens Point
- UW-Green Bay
- UW-Fox Valley
- UW-Manitowoc
- UW-Oshkosh
- UW-La Crosse
- UW-Fond du Lac
- UW-Sheboygan
- UW-Baraboo/Sauk County
- UW-Washington County
- UW-Richland
- UW-Madison
- UW-Milwaukee
- UW-Waukesha
- UW-Platteville
- UW-Whitewater
- UW-Rock County
- UW-Parkside

■ Universities
● Freshman-Sophomore Colleges
UW-Extension Offices in every county

Map courtesy of the UW System

Protecting Our Resources

Wisconsin has outstanding natural resources: beautiful forests, lakes and streams, and fish and game. Our state also has valuable mineral resources, such as iron ore, limestone, and lead. But these resources must be shared among all people. These resources must be used carefully so they may continue to be enjoyed by everyone. The Wisconsin Department of Natural Resources (DNR) must make sure that these resources are protected and available for everyone—even future

industrial: To do with businesses and factories

generations—to enjoy. The DNR protects forests, wildlife, water, and land from pollution and misuse. The DNR also makes sure that sporting activities like hunting and fishing are done fairly and in a way that will not harm either the animal population or their natural habitat.

Travel Around the State

Because we have so many beautiful natural places, **tourism** (**tur** izm) is very important to Wisconsin, and a state Department of Tourism promotes travel to Wisconsin. The Department of Tourism operates travel information centers where visitors can learn more about where to go in the state. The DNR also creates advertisements and publications. These are sent to other states to encourage people to visit Wisconsin.

Traveling around the state requires good roads. In 1911, the legislature created the State Highway **Commission** (cuh **mih** shun) to help build public highways. More and more people began driving automobiles on roads and highways.

Forests, like this one in Flambeau State Park, are one of Wisconsin's great natural resources.
WHi (X3) 27761

WHS Archives, Pamphlet Collection

Travel booklets, such as this one, used Wisconsin's natural resources to attract tourists to the state.

The state recognized a need to promote safe driving and ensure that all drivers knew how to drive safely. Today, the Department of Transportation does all these things. It plans and constructs roads and highways, promotes highway safety, enforces traffic laws through the state patrol, licenses drivers, and registers automobiles. All of these functions are important to keep us safe on the roads.

Keeping Business Safe and Fair

When you buy food at the grocery store, you expect that it is safe to eat, right? And your parents expect that when they buy a new car it will run. Ensuring that Wisconsin **consumers** are treated fairly is the job of the Department of Agriculture, Trade, and Consumer Protection. Protection of Wisconsin's agriculture and commerce began even before Wisconsin was a state. Since agriculture has always been important in the state, this protection began with farm products. In 1839, the territorial assembly required every county to have an inspector. The inspector made sure the food products, like milk and cheese, were wholesome and safe.

An agricultural inspector carefully inspects an ear of corn.

WHS Archives

WHi Image ID 2039

Wisconsin makes sure its cheese is always good!

consumers: People who buy goods or services

Since the 1970s, the Department of Agriculture, Trade and Consumer Protection has also protected more than just our food. The department prevents false advertising and unsafe products. It creates rules that protect consumers from people who might produce or sell goods and services unfairly.

Looking Back

Wisconsin's government does much more than just pass and enforce laws. When we all work together, we can provide many opportunities for everybody. State government provides education from public kindergartens through higher education at the university level. Government also makes sure that the resources we enjoy today—like parks and forests—are still there in the future.

Graphic by Amelia Janes, Midwest Educational Graphics

State government works for Wisconsin citizens in many ways.

Government also makes sure everyone is treated fairly. Government agencies protect us in many areas of our lives, such as work and food safety. State government also serves Wisconsin citizens in many ways beyond those highlighted in this chapter. Different agencies protect workers, those out of work, and others, such as the disabled and sick, who need special help.

These students at the State School for the Deaf worked on math problems in 1893.

The Wisconsin School for the Blind in Janesville, 1893

County board inspecting East De Pere Road between Green Bay and De Pere in the early 1900s

The kitchen at Mendota Mental Health Hospital about 100 years ago

Workers building a bridge over the Wolf River on the Wisconsin and Northern Railroad in Neopit, 1907

Chapter 5
Local Government

In Chapter 4, you discovered the many things governments can do. Providing education and protecting natural resources makes our lives better. But the state government cannot do everything. And we really would not be happy if the state controlled *all* the decisions that governments make. Wisconsin is a large state. Its citizens have many different needs.

What the people of Milwaukee need or want might be very different from what the people of Rusk County need or want. This is why local government is so important. Government at the local level allows people to decide for themselves what services to provide and how to solve problems that affect only their communities. Having more levels of government gives people more freedom to do what they want.

WHi Image ID 3787

Local governments pave roads like this one in Racine, 1901.

70

There are 2 basic kinds of local governments: county and **municipal** (myoo **niss** uh puhl). The entire state of Wisconsin is divided into 72 counties. Think about it. *Every* part of the state is also part of a county.

Municipal governments are smaller units of government. They include cities, villages, and towns. Municipal governments are different depending on how many people live in a place. Cities are the largest, governing the greatest number of people living close together. Villages are like very small cities. Towns govern fewer people spread out over a large area. As of 2002, Wisconsin had 190 cities, 395 villages, and 1,265 towns. Each type of local government has different responsibilities and provides important services to its people.

In some ways, your school is similar. The state sets some rules that all schools must follow. And your school district sets rules that schools in your district must follow. In this way the school district is like the county level of government. But your school and even your classroom can set its own rules, too. They function like municipal governments. Just like your classroom and your school, local governments let people make many decisions for themselves.

Questions to Think About

How do more levels of government give us more freedom? How is local government different from state government? What does county government do? What responsibilities are left up to **municipalities** (myoo nih sih **pal** ih teez)? How is city government similar to state government?

municipal: To do with a city or town and its services, such as municipal workers   **municipalities:** Towns, villages, or cities

County Government

When Wisconsin Territory was created in 1836, there were only 4 counties covering what is now the state of Wisconsin. The territory was divided into quarters, with Brown County in the northeast, Crawford County in the northwest, Iowa County in the southwest, and Milwaukee County in the southeast. A few people lived across the largest area. More people lived in the southern part of Wisconsin Territory.

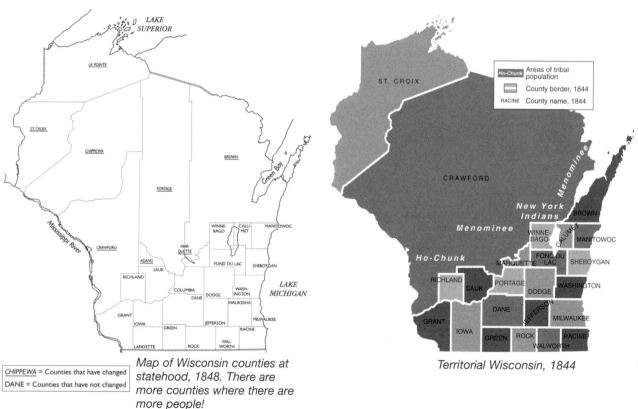

Map of Wisconsin counties at statehood, 1848. There are more counties where there are more people!

CHIPPEWA = Counties that have changed
DANE = Counties that have not changed

Territorial Wisconsin, 1844

Then, a growing population required more services. They needed law enforcement and **surveying**. Soon, the territorial legislature created more counties. When Wisconsin became a state, there were 29 counties. All but 9 counties were south of the Fox-Wisconsin Riverway, since that was where most of the people lived.

The number of counties continued to grow. By 1861, there were 58 counties. Between 1861 and 1901, 13 new counties were created in northern Wisconsin. That's when lumberjacks cleared the forests and farmers settled on the land. The last county, Menominee, was created in 1961. It includes the entire Menominee Indian Reservation.

Counties serve 2 important functions. First, they carry out duties required by the state at the county level. For example, the residents of the county elect the sheriff and district attorney. They enforce state law through the sheriff's department and through the court. Each county has its own court and courthouse where people accused of breaking the law are tried. No one has to travel to Madison to appear in court.

WHS Archives, Classified File 5536

Clearing forests created jobs for lumberjacks in the late 1800s and brought new settlers to northern Wisconsin.

The state also needs county-by-county information about people throughout the state. So each county also keeps **records** (**rek** urds) about the people living there, such as circuit court records and tax records. The courthouse makes these records easily available when people need them.

surveying: To determine the form, extent, and position of a piece of land by measuring   **records:** Facts written down to keep as official documents

73

Wisconsin was the first state to create a numbering system to direct highway traffic. You can see the road sign on the bridge in this photo.

RURAL HIGHWAYS

Poor roads put the family "in a rut" and keep it there.

Good roads mean opportunity for
1 Neighborhood social life
2 Consolidated schools
3 Prompt mail service
4 Church attendance
5 Prompt medical attendance
6 Cheaper hauling of produce

Second, counties allow the people to govern themselves and provide services that are needed in local areas. The most familiar responsibility is transportation. Counties construct and maintain roads, called "County Trunk Highways," (CTH) named after letters (like CTH Q in Taylor County). Every winter, county road crews plow the roads and make sure they are safe to drive.

Every county has a sheriff and deputies to enforce laws and help people in trouble. Many counties also run employment centers to help people find jobs. Counties have health offices to help people with physical and mental illnesses. Often, counties construct and maintain county parks and other recreational areas. These services are paid for by property taxes. Every homeowner in the county pays taxes to the government. Tax rates vary from county to county. Based on the needs and wants of the people, each county can decide what services to provide. Counties also decide how much money to raise to pay for such services.

How do good roads keep travelers safe?

Counties vary in size and population. Marathon is the largest of Wisconsin's 72 counties in land area. Ozaukee, on the shore of Lake Michigan, is the smallest. The largest in terms of population is Milwaukee County. And the smallest is Menominee County. Population growth rates differ as well. In northern, mostly rural counties the number of people stays about the same from year to year. Other counties, like Waukesha and Dane, are growing rapidly. More and more people move to them every year.

Green County sheriff's badge, 1900–1905

WHS Museum: 1970.233.4

Each county is divided into districts of equal population, like the state assembly and senate. Each district elects a supervisor to sit on the board. Supervisors in most counties serve 2-year terms, but in Milwaukee they serve 4-year terms.

Counties also have an executive branch of government, but it varies from county to county. In some counties, the people elect a county executive who works much like the governor. In other counties, the board of supervisors appoints a county **administrator** (ad **mihn** uh stra tur). In still other counties, the board of supervisors simply picks one of its own members to lead meetings, communicate with the state, and manage the county government. These county officials have much less power than county executives and can only carry out the duties given by the board of supervisors.

administrator: Someone who controls something

75

WISCONSIN'S "LITTLE CAPITOLS"

Every county has a courthouse located in the county seat. You may have visited your county courthouse with your parents. Courthouses come in all shapes and sizes. The oldest courthouse in Wisconsin is in Grant County. It was designed to look like a Greek temple, which was a very popular style in the 1840s and 1850s. Taylor County's courthouse in Medford is a large brick building with a copper dome. Racine County's courthouse looks like a little skyscraper. No matter what these buildings look like, they are important centers of government for counties.

Baraboo County courthouse

Grant County courthouse

Photos by Jim Drager, WHS Historic Preservation

WHS Archives, Classified File 672

Meetings are important ways for citizens to learn about issues in their communities and to voice their opinions.

Each county has a "county seat." This is where the business of government is located and is home to the county courthouse. The courthouse is where county records are kept. People pay their property taxes at the courthouse, and the circuit court meets there. Often, the courthouse is also where you'll find the sheriff's department and other county officials, including the board of supervisors. The county courthouse is like a little capitol building for the county. What offices are in the courthouse in your county?

Municipal Government for Cities, Villages, and Towns

Wisconsin has 3 different kinds of municipal government: cities, villages, and towns. Municipal governments are created to serve the needs of a large number of people living close together. They provide services like counties do, but for a smaller area and often for more people. Municipal government first appeared in Wisconsin in 1821 with the establishment of Prairie du Chien. In 1848, Wisconsin had so few people that there were only about a dozen villages and one city—Milwaukee.

Cities are units of government for small areas with a large population. Even so, there is great variety among cities' populations. Wisconsin's largest city is Milwaukee. In 2000, nearly 600,000 people lived in Milwaukee. The smallest city is Bayfield, with a population of only 611 people.

Major Cities in Wisconsin

LAKE SUPERIOR

Superior

Wausau

Eau Claire

Stevens Point

Green Bay

Mississippi River

Appleton

Neenah

Oshkosh

Manitowoc

La Crosse

Fond du Lac

Sheboygan

LAKE MICHIGAN

West Bend

Wauwatosa

Watertown

Menomonee Falls

Madison

Brookfield

Waukesha

Milwaukee

New Berlin

West Allis

Franklin

Janesville

Greenfield

Racine

Beloit

Kenosha

• Cities of more than 20,000 people

WISCONSIN'S TOP TEN CITIES

Wisconsin has 190 cities that range in population from nearly 600,000 to just over 600. Below is a list of Wisconsin's 10 largest cities as of the year 2000.

Milwaukee: 596,974

Madison: 208,054

Green Bay: 102,779

Kenosha: 90,352

Racine: 81,855

Appleton: 70,087

Waukesha: 64,825

Oshkosh: 62,916

Eau Claire: 61,704

West Allis: 61,254

How big is your nearest city?

Green Bay, 1893

Washburn, 1886

People who live close together need to cooperate and share resources much more than people who live far apart. When a large number of people, usually at least 1,000, live in a small area, they often decide to **incorporate** (in **cor** pur ate) into a city. Cities provide more services and govern themselves with greater independence from the state or county. For example, in rural areas, most houses have their own wells for drinking water and their own septic systems for sewage. But when many people build houses close together, there are too many wells too close together to be safe. So cities operate a water system and a sewer system that provides everybody with clean drinking water and treats waste.

An early picture of the Prairie du Chien Fire Department

Living close together also requires more cooperation for public safety. Most cities have police departments to enforce the laws. And most cities have fire departments to fight fires. Fires can spread rapidly in neighborhoods with lots of houses. When many people live closely together, the streets must be built and kept in good repair. The government also collects garbage and recyclable materials so that these items do not pile up as trash in people's yards and cause health problems.

What else do cities need to do for themselves? Most cities maintain parks or other places for people to play and enjoy themselves. City government also works to keep things fair. Most cities have **zoning** and building **regulations** that separate neighborhoods from factories and other noisy and dangerous places. Building regulations also prevent someone from constructing a building that is unsafe. It could endanger other buildings and people in the neighborhood.

zoning: Keeping one area separate from another, such as businesses and houses **regulations:** Official rules or orders   79

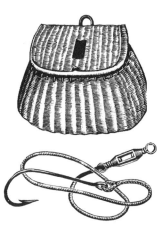

How do cities govern themselves and decide what rules are fair? Cities have the same 3 branches of government that the state does. A city is divided into **wards** . Then one or more wards are combined into **aldermanic** (al dur **man** ic) districts. Each aldermanic district is equal in population, and voters elect an **alder** , or representative, to the city council. The city council is like the legislative branch of city government. The city council passes laws, called **ordinances** (**or** dih nun suhs), to govern the city.

City parks, like Tenney Park in Madison, are places for people to relax and enjoy nature.

WHi (M492) 430

Voters in a city elect the mayor or city manager to head the executive branch. The mayor or city manager's job is to run the different departments of city government and to make sure that the laws are enforced. Just like the governor, a mayor or city manager needs the help of other elected officials to make government serve the people's needs. These jobs include a city clerk to keep records and a treasurer to manage the city's money.

wards: Places where people vote   **ordinances:** Laws issued by a governmental authority

Many cities also have a judicial branch of government, as well. Cooperation requires that everyone follow the same set of rules. Municipal courts try people who break city ordinances, like parking in an unsafe place or speeding. People who break ordinances often must pay a fine to the city.

A public library is another service of local government that everyone is able to enjoy.

Villages operate a lot like cities, only with a much smaller population. When a few hundred people live close together, they still need services similar to those in a city. But villages do not need as many people to provide those services, so their governments are smaller.

Villages have a board of trustees, usually consisting of 3–6 members who are elected by the people. Rather than representing a separate district, each trustee represents the village as a whole. Villages do not have mayors, but one of the trustees serves as the board president. He or she runs board meetings, makes sure that laws are enforced, and makes sure services are provided. Villages may provide the same services as cities but on a much smaller scale.

Towns are the third form of local government. Every part of the state not governed by a village or a city is governed under a town form of government. This means that most towns are rural. The town form of government was brought to Wisconsin by settlers from New England. It is the most democratic form of local government since the legislative body is the "town meeting."

At annual town meetings, all voting citizens meet to approve local laws and the budget. Everybody is part of the government! The day-to-day business of towns is carried out by a town board, usually made up of 3 supervisors. Towns have elected officials, including a clerk and a treasurer.

Towns are large in area and small in population. So the most important function of town government is maintaining roads. Town roads connect rural areas and allow people to travel safely. Towns may also operate centers for people to bring their waste materials to recycle. Larger towns may also provide some limited fire and police services to keep people safe. In places where people live closer together, the town might adopt zoning and building regulations similar to cities or villages. These regulations protect the environment as well as the people.

Looking Back

Government does not just exist in the state capital of Madison but begins on your own doorstep! Local government is very important in Wisconsin. Local government allows people greater ability to govern themselves. It provides services that differ from place to place, depending upon the people's needs.

Everyone lives within 2 forms of local government: one county and one municipal—a city, village, or town. Local governments assist the state government by enforcing laws and keeping important records. They also allow people to decide what kinds of services they need or want, such as clean drinking water, libraries, or parks. Local government is all about neighbors working together to take care of each other. Learn about who runs the government where you live!

CALEDONIA FAIR!

The Caledonia and Vicinity Annual Fair

will take place on TUESDAY the 2d day of October, 1860, on the premises of Thomas Robertson, Esq., Farmer, Caledonia.

The prizes will be awarded on the ground at the close of the Exhibition.

An Address is expected to be delivered by the

HON. A. SCOTT SLOAN,

J. GRAY, Secretary.   J. S. RICHMOND, President.

Top: Many counties hold fairs where people can enjoy food and entertainment. This is the Sauk County Fair in 1906.

Bottom: Poster for a fair in Caledonia, 1860

83

Chapter 6

Who Are the Voters in Wisconsin?

★ ★ ★

Is your school a democracy? Probably not. In a democracy, the people rule themselves through elected officials like the governor or members of the legislature. But you and your classmates do not choose your teachers and principal. The principal and teachers work to make the school a place where students will enjoy learning. But these adults make all the decisions about what *they* feel students need for their education. They are the experts. This kind of decision-making works fine for a school, but in a democracy like Wisconsin, the people need to rule themselves.

Who are "we, the people"? We all are!

In a democracy, the people who rule themselves do so by electing those they want to govern them. The people who rule themselves are the voters. But who can vote? The answer to that question has changed many times since Wisconsin became a state.

84

All people have to obey the law. But people cannot really take an active role in our democracy unless the government can hear their voices. And voting is one of the best ways that people make their voices heard. In this chapter, you will see how ideas about who can vote have changed over time. People now included were first **excluded** (ex **clu** duhd) from the right to vote.

Think back to Chapter 2, when people in Wisconsin were writing and voting on a constitution. Many people then living here were not counted as voters. Remember that those allowed to vote did not include many people who can vote in Wisconsin today. There are 3 groups who were excluded. In 1848, no women, no African American men, and no male members of Wisconsin Indian Nations were allowed to vote.

Voting in an election in Menominee Falls, 1980

Questions to Think About

Why have our ideas changed since statehood about who should be **eligible** (**el** uh juh buhl) to vote? Why is the right to vote so important? How did women, African Americans, and members of American Indian Nations finally get the right to vote? Why did it take each group such a long time to gain this right?

---

excluded: Left out   **eligible:** Able or having the right qualifications to do something

Defining "the People"

In Chapter 2, you learned that the people's rights and responsibilities were written down in the Wisconsin Constitution. The constitution begins "We, the people of Wisconsin. . . ." But, at the time that it was written, the constitution also limited those who had the right to vote.

Article 3 of the constitution defined **electors**, or those people who can vote. In order to vote in Wisconsin, a person had to be 21 years old and a man. If you were younger than 21 or a woman, you had no voice in making the laws. But you still had to obey all of them.

You also had to be white. In 1848, there were about 1,000 African Americans living in Wisconsin. They, too, had to obey all the laws. But they could not vote. They had no voice in government.

WHi (X3) 12008

To vote, a person also needed to be a citizen of the United States. People born in the United States are natural citizens. People born in another country can be **naturalized** (**nach** ur uh lized). That is, they can study to become citizens. Of course, only naturalized white men could vote.

Even in 1902, the constitution still limited who could participate in government. There are only men at this De Pere City Council meeting.

Most Wisconsin Indians were not allowed to vote, since they lived under tribal law. Only those Indians who lived outside the reservation, owned property, and paid taxes like their non-Indian neighbors could vote.

So African Americans, women, and most Wisconsin Indians had no voice in state government. Of course, the legislature, the governor, and the supreme court still had to protect these people. African Americans, women, and most Wisconsin Indians still had other rights described in the constitution. But when groups have no voice in government, it becomes easy for the government to overlook them.

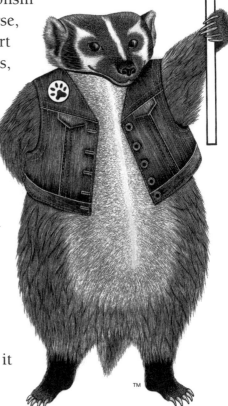

At any time, the legislature could pass a law that would give a group of people, such as women or African Americans, the right to vote. Citizens would also have to vote to support such a change.

Sooner or later, the groups who were denied the right to vote demanded to be fully included in "the people." Women, African Americans, and Native people worked to get the right to vote. But it wasn't easy. And it didn't happen quickly.

Women Demand the Right to Vote

The Wisconsin Constitution denied women the right to vote. But Wisconsin was not alone. No state allowed women to vote in state elections until the 1890s.

Women who led the fight for the right to vote (also know as **suffrage** [**suh** frahj]) were called **suffragists** (**suh** frah jists). Suffragists held conventions in Janesville in 1867 and in Milwaukee in 1869. Some of these women organized the Wisconsin Woman Suffrage Association and set up local chapters in many cities. But they were not very successful. The suffrage leaders seemed unable to get the public to accept that women could do more than raise children and cook meals.

WOMEN ORGANIZE TO VOTE

In 1848, Wisconsin became a state. That same year, Elizabeth Cady Stanton and Susan B. Anthony organized a large meeting in Seneca Falls, New York. This meeting was the beginning of a nationwide movement to allow women to vote. Women were active in **reform** movements. Women worked to fight against slavery, for example. But there was little support for giving women the right to vote.

WHi Image ID 8235

Susan B. Anthony and Elizabeth Cady Stanton, 1891

Suffragists finally had some success in 1885. That year, the legislature passed a bill giving women the right to vote in school elections. But they could not vote in other elections. Many people still believed that a woman's place was in the home. But this law gave women some say over their children's schooling.

reform: Working to change things for the better

But women did not stop. For years they argued that the right to vote should be extended equally to both men and women. Beginning in the 1890s, more and more women began to argue that it was even more important for women to vote than men!

How could women take care of their children if factories polluted the water and air? How could they take care of their homes without voting on city issues like sewage and water services? Women felt that they needed to have a voice in larger community concerns. In other words, women had to argue that they needed to vote in order to take care of the community as if it were their own family!

I WILL VOTE

Suffragists had to be demanding! Just look at how this woman on this poster is standing!

After years of hard work, suffragists at last succeeded in getting a bill passed by the legislature that would grant them full voting rights. The final challenge was that voters would have to approve the measure in November 1912. In the months before the vote,

THE REVEREND OLYMPIA BROWN

One of the leading suffragists in Wisconsin was Olympia Brown (1835–1926). She was born on a farm in Michigan and worked hard to become a minister. She was only the second woman minister in the United States. In 1878, she moved to Racine and carried on her work as a minister and as president of the Wisconsin Woman Suffrage Association.

Olympia Brown

BELLE CASE LA FOLLETTE

Belle Case La Follette (1859–1931) was the wife of Wisconsin's progressive governor Robert M. La Follette (lah **fah** let) and worked for women's suffrage. She graduated from the University of Wisconsin in 1879 and married Robert M. La Follette in 1881. In 1885, she became the first woman to receive a degree from the UW Law School. Belle La Follette also wrote articles for newspapers and magazines.

Belle Case La Follette talking to farmers about women's suffrage, about 1915

Many women across the state and country participated in the suffrage movement.

suffragists traveled around the state. They mailed thousands of pamphlets to voters, urging them to support suffrage for women. Suffragists went to every county fair and all kinds of meetings. They hoped voters would understand that women deserved the right to vote. When Wisconsin voted, 135,545 people voted to give women the right to vote, but 227,024 voted against it!

By 1900, even more younger suffragists had grown up. They included

META BERGER

Like Belle Case La Follette, Meta Schlichting Berger (1873–1944) worked for reform in Wisconsin. Her husband was Victor Berger, a Milwaukee newspaper editor, mayor, and congressman. Meta Berger taught school in Milwaukee. In 1909 she was elected to the Milwaukee School Board. Meta Berger was one of the first women to be elected to public office in the state! She served on the school board for 30 years, and suggested ideas like school lunches and free textbooks. Meta Berger was also active in the women's suffrage movement.

In the early 1900s Meta Berger added her voice to work for suffrage.

★ Belle Case La Follette, the first woman to receive a law degree from the University of Wisconsin;

★ Ada James, wife of a Wisconsin senator;

★ Meta Berger, wife of Milwaukee's mayor; and

★ Theodora Youmans, wife of the editor of the *Freeman,* a Waukesha newspaper. Suffragists in Wisconsin marched in parades and spent much time and money to convince people that women should have the right to vote.

It was a bitter disappointment when people voted against the bill in 1912. But suffragists kept working. The victory finally was won not in Wisconsin but on a national level. First, in 1919, suffragists convinced members of Congress to approve an amendment to the U.S. Constitution. This amendment guaranteed women the right to vote.

Next, suffragists had to convince the legislatures in at least 36 states. They had to officially approve the amendment before it could become part of the constitution. In June 1919 the Wisconsin legislature approved the suffrage amendment.

> "No. No. No. Never.—No decent woman can or will allow herself to stoop so low as to enter politics. Politics are dirty and if women enter they will be dirtier....No 'real woman' wants to vote."

Ada James, a Wisconsin suffragist, received this response from a Milwaukee newspaper editor when she asked him to feature pro-suffrage news in 1912.

A special messenger rushed the formal papers to the Secretary of State in Washington, D.C. By a matter of minutes, Wisconsin became the first state to **ratify** (**rat** ih fye) the 19th Amendment. In 1920, the 19th Amendment gave women across the nation the right to vote.

Women still continued to face **discrimination** (dis krim uh **na** shun). They had a hard time finding jobs. They were often paid less than men doing the same work.

Although women could vote, only a few women served in the legislature. Wisconsin voters did not elect a woman to a statewide office until 1960. That's when Dena A. Smith was elected state treasurer. Not until 1982 was the constitution amended to read "all *people* are born free and independent," instead of "all *men*." Wisconsin did not send a woman to Congress until 1998. That's when Tammy Baldwin was elected to the House of Representatives. In 2004, Wisconsin voters elected the first African American woman, Gwendolyn Moore, to represent the state.

La Crosse Tribune and Leader Press

Local Weather

The La Crosse Tribune
and Leader-Press

Full Leased Wire News Report of the Associated Press

Evening Edition · TEN PAGES ·

Member of the Audit Bureau of Circulation

VOLUME XVI, NUMBER 21　　LA CROSSE, WISCONSIN, THURSDAY, JUNE 5, 1919　　PRICE THREE CENTS

EQUAL SUFFRAGE RESOLUTION PASSES SENATE

Wisconsin was the first state to ratify the 19th Amendment.

　　ratify: To agree or to approve officially　　**discrimination:** Unfair treatment of people, based on differences such as race, age, or place of birth

African Americans' Struggle for the Vote

In Chapter 2 you learned that in 1847 Wisconsin voters refused to give African Americans the right to vote. People who believed African Americans *should* have the right to vote tried again. In 1849, the legislature passed a law to give African American men the right to vote. But this time very few people bothered to vote. Since only about 17 out of every 100 people voted to give African Americans the right to vote, election officials ruled that the **referendum** (ref uh **ren** duhm) failed. Once again, African American men were denied the right to vote.

African Americans continued to protest. At a meeting in Milwaukee in 1855, a large group demanded that the legislature again try to grant them the right to vote. The legislature heard their demand and put the question to the people 2 more times, in 1857 and in 1865. But both times, people voted down these attempts to give African American men the right to vote. No matter how unfair it seems to us today, voters at that time just did not want African Americans to have that right.

Even though Martha and Notley Henderson were early settlers in Madison, male African Americans were not allowed to vote until 1866. African American women could not vote until the 19th Amendment was ratified in 1919.

WHi Image ID 4175

---

referendum: A vote by the people on a public measure

Ezekiel Gillespie
WHi (X3) 32541

Then a remarkable thing happened. In the 1865 election, one of the people who was denied the right to vote was **Ezekiel** (ee zee kee **uhl**) Gillespie, an African American living in Milwaukee. When his **ballot** was refused on election day, Gillespie **sued** the election officials. He insisted that he should have the right to vote.

Gillespie's case went before the Wisconsin Supreme Court the following year, in 1866. The 3 justices of the supreme court considered the matter. They agreed that Gillespie and all African American men in the state could vote.

The supreme court's decision made many people very angry. Although some people threatened to use force to keep African American men from voting, African Americans refused to be scared off. In 1866, many African Americans voted for the first time. And the election was peaceful.

Although the right to vote is one of the most important rights, it does not guarantee that all citizens will be treated equally. African American men won the vote in 1866, but still suffered discrimination. They still do.

ballot: A secret way of voting, such as on a machine or on a slip of paper   **sued:** Started a legal case against someone in a court of law

American Indians and the Question of Citizenship

The Wisconsin Constitution recognized 2 groups of Wisconsin Indians differently. Those who lived on reservations as members of tribes were *not* given the right to vote, even though they lived in Wisconsin. But the Wisconsin Indians who had taken up farming among non-Indian settlers and lived *separately* from their Nations were given the right to vote.

To the framers of the constitution, this decision seemed sound. The framers felt that the Indians who lived like their non-Indian neighbors would be included in "We, the people." The members of Indian Nations who lived the traditional Indian life on the reservations were not considered part of "We, the people."

The government also divided tribal reservation land among individual Indians. Then the government sold the rest of the

Sewing class at the Lac du Flambeau school for Indian children, 1895. Native children were forced to attend government boarding schools. The students could not speak their traditional languages. And they were taught only skills that could lead to low-paying jobs in the non-Indian world.

reservation land to non-Indian settlers. These actions hurt the Indian people. And they still had no voice in the government, since most Native people were not U.S. citizens and could not vote.

The turning point in American Indian citizenship came during World War I (1914–1918). Because American Indians were not U.S. citizens, they could not be made to fight in the war. Yet many Native men signed up, especially those from Wisconsin.

Even though American Indians were not U.S. citizens, many signed up to fight in World War I.

After the 19th Amendment gave women the right to vote, many people thought it unfair that American Indians did not have this right as well. Many Native men had fought and died for their country in World War I. In 1924, Congress passed the Indian Citizenship Act. This act finally made *all* American Indians citizens and gave them the right to vote. Since the 19th Amendment had already passed, American Indian women could also vote. But even though they could vote, American Indians still faced discrimination.

But Wisconsin Indian Nations continued to struggle to let the government and others know about their sovereignty rights and their culture. Reservations remained poor places for many years, with poor schools and poor housing.

When members of Ojibwe bands began spearfishing in the 1970s, they faced protests from non-Indians. The non-Indians were angry at the Ojibwes' attempts to follow their treaty rights.

Spearfishing is an important treaty right of the Ojibwe people.

The courts finally supported the Ojibwe bands' treaty rights. The courts ruled that the Ojibwe bands had the right to fish, gather, and hunt on land off of their reservations.

The development of tribal gaming has brought more money to reservations. Wisconsin Indians have used this money to build schools, health clinics, day care centers, and housing. But American Indians continue to face unfair treatment.

Look at the faces of the people and the signs in this anti-treaty rights cartoon from the Milwaukee Journal, April 28, 1989.

Looking Back

The most important right we have is the right to vote. It is also a great responsibility. A vote is a voice in a democracy. So getting to vote is the most important part of being one of "We the people." The Wisconsin Constitution first allowed only white men to vote. Over time, the actions of many women, African Americans, and Wisconsin Indians forced the state to recognize that they, too, were part of "We the people." All people deserved to have a say in government. After many years of struggle, *all* adult members of these groups finally won the right to vote.

Indian and non-Indian fisheries make sure that there are healthy fish to catch.

Chapter 7
Political Parties and Elections

★ ★ ★

Children learning about voting

Do you belong to any special groups? Perhaps you play on a soccer team that meets every week for practice or a game. Or maybe you get together with a group of your friends to play video games. Or you might belong to a scout troop or a swim team. Adults like to form and join organized clubs, too. Some of these clubs, like the Lions Club or the Rotary Club, do good things for the community. Others, like quilt groups or groups of Packer Backers, allow people to do things together with other people who share the same interests.

Many adults belong to a kind of group known as a **political** (pah **lih** tih kuhl) party. A political party is an organization made up of people who share similar ideas of what government should do. Political parties have a special part to play in elections. Remember that in a democracy, people vote to elect their leaders in government.

WHS Archives, Classified File 3775, Milwaukee Journal photo by Carol Hoyt

Political parties are very important in elections. The political party helps **candidates** (**can** dih duts), those people running for office, get elected. Political parties do 3 things to help candidates get elected. First, a political party **nominates** (**nahm** in ates) a candidate for a particular office. Next, the party educates the voters about the **campaign** (cam **pane**). Then the party works to make the candidate known to the people who will be voting. People often vote for a candidate because of that candidate's political party.

Representative Lena Taylor being sworn into office

Questions to Think About

What do political parties do? What are the major political parties in Wisconsin? Who is one of the most important political leaders in our state's history? How do elections—national, state, and local—work in Wisconsin? What's the difference between a primary election and a general election?

People registering to vote many years ago

nominates: Suggests that someone would be the right person to do a job or to receive an honor   **campaign:** A series of actions and activities, organized over time, to win something, like an election

Political Parties in Wisconsin

Candidates running for office in the fall elections are **partisan** (**par** tih zun) candidates. That is, they belong to a political party and agree with the views shared by the members of that party. There have been many different political parties in Wisconsin since statehood. Some political parties, like the **Republican** (re **pub** luh cun) Party and the **Democratic** Party, have been around for a long time and are still strong. Other political parties were strong for a few years and then faded away. Still others, like the **Green** Party, are much newer. The members of all of these parties meet regularly. When they meet, they create a statement of what they think about the important problems of the day. This statement is called a **platform**.

Political Parties in Wisconsin History

Before statehood, Wisconsin had 2 main parties: the Democrats and the **Whigs**. Right after Wisconsin became a state in 1848, the problem of slavery in the United States grew larger and larger. Democrats felt that each state should make its own decision whether or not people living there could own slaves. Whigs were divided on the question of what to do about slavery. Some Whigs believed that the United States should **abolish** (ah **bahl** ish) slavery. Other Whigs did not agree with this.

"Vote Democratic" donkey lapel tag
WHS Museum: 1965.237.71

The Republican Party Is Born

In 1854 many people in Wisconsin who were against slavery gathered in Ripon. Some were Whigs and some were not. They got together to organize a new political party. They named their party the Republican Party. The Republicans officially

abolish: Do away with

Schoolhouse in Ripon, Wisconsin, where the Republican party was born

opposed slavery. Many people in Wisconsin agreed with the Republicans. By 1860, most of the people who were elected to state government were members of the Republican Party. The Democrats also remained powerful, but the Whigs disappeared.

Meetings similar to the one held in Ripon occurred in other states. Soon people organized a national Republican Party. In 1860, the Republicans elected Abraham Lincoln president. During the Civil War, most Wisconsin citizens fought to oppose the spread of slavery. The Republican Party remained powerful in Wisconsin for the rest of the 1800s.

Republican State Convention ribbon, 1936
WHS Museum: 1986.293.1

The Progressives

The most successful political effort in the early 1900s was the **Progressive** (pro **greh** siv) movement. Progressives supported progress or positive change. Do you remember reading about Belle Case La Follette in Chapter 6? Her husband was known as "Fighting Bob" La Follette. The Progressive movement was formed in the 1890s when "Fighting Bob" La Follette led a fight within the Republican Party. He wanted to make the Republican Party and the state government more willing to answer to the people of the state. For many years the Progressives remained a separate group within the Republican Party.

Rally for Progressive candidate Robert M. La Follette Jr., 1936

WHi (X3) 22749

In 1900, after years of bitter fighting, La Follette was elected governor. He served until 1906, when he became a U.S. Senator. Under La Follette and other Progressive governors, Wisconsin passed a number of laws that made people's lives better. People all over the country recognized Wisconsin for making state government more democratic.

The Progressives made businesses and industries treat employees more fairly. And the Progressives made sure that businesses charged fair prices and had safe working conditions. Progressives also wanted to help people in other ways. In 1911, Wisconsin created the nation's first workers' **compensation** (com pen **sa** shun) program to assist workers who were hurt on the job. In 1932, Wisconsin created the nation's first unemployment compensation program, to help people who lost their jobs.

In 1934, Progressives formally left the Republican Party and formed a separate, independent party. Progressives elected Robert M. La Follette's sons, Philip F. La Follette and Robert M. La Follette Jr., governor and U.S. Senator. Progressives also elected many members of the legislature. Progressives sent many representatives to Congress.

Wisconsin Progressive Conference ribbon, 1934

WHS Museum: 1980.22728

compensation: Something that makes up for something else, such as a loss or injury

Political Parties in Wisconsin Today

After early success, support for the Progressive Party began to drop in the 1940s. Many of its younger members joined the Democratic Party. Since the 1950s, Wisconsin politics has been fairly equally balanced between the Democratic and Republican Parties.

Wisconsin Libertarian Party button
WHS Museum: 1988.214.1

Other political parties still exist, however. When some voters feel that the Democrats and Republicans do not pay attention to things that are important to them, they organize new political parties. Today, the 2 other important parties in Wisconsin are the **Libertarian** (lib ur **tehr** ee uhn) Party and the Wisconsin Green Party.

Members of the Libertarian Party believe that government has become too powerful and that people should have more freedom. They want to limit the role of government involvement in areas such as education, transportation, and health care.

WHS Archives, Heimann-Winske

Republican convention in Oshkosh, May 4, 1946

The Wisconsin Green Party formed originally to increase government protection of the environment. Although environmental protection is still a large part of their platform, Greens also want to increase state spending on education, health care, and agriculture.

103

Elections in Wisconsin

In earlier chapters you learned that in a democracy, people elect the officials who serve in government. Some of these officials become governor or members of the legislature. Every year, voters in Wisconsin participate in several elections to choose their elected officials. Elections occur in the spring and in the fall and are usually divided into 2 types, the primary election and the general election.

Fall Elections

The main difference between the spring and fall elections is that the fall elections are partisan. This means that candidates in the fall elections run as members of one of Wisconsin's political parties. Republicans and Democrats are the 2 biggest parties. Each party holds a primary election first.

Before the primary election, people who want to run for office begin asking others to sign their **nomination** (nahm uh **na** shun) papers. If they receive enough signatures from supporters, then those who want to run for office formally become candidates. Their names will appear on the ballot.

104   **nomination:** Being chosen to run for office or to receive an honor or job

WHY DO WE HAVE PRIMARY AND GENERAL ELECTIONS?

You may be wondering why we have both primary elections and general elections. Robert M. "Fighting Bob" La Follette was probably the most famous political leader in Wisconsin history. He pushed for primary elections over 100 years ago.

Before La Follette's Progressive movement in the 1890s, candidates for the November elections were not chosen in an election. They were chosen during a convention of party members sent by their local parties. Only a few people were involved in selecting candidates. That means a powerful and wealthy group of men could select whom they wanted.

WHi Image ID 5455

La Follette believed he was the popular choice for governor in 1896 and 1898. But powerful men didn't want him nominated. When the convention was held, they made sure that La Follette didn't get the nomination.

Robert M. La Follette. Can you see why he was nicknamed, "Fighting Bob"?

Finally, when La Follette was elected governor in 1900, he wanted to end the unfair way candidates were chosen. He, and others like him, felt that the citizens needed a more democratic way to choose their candidates. In 1905, Wisconsin passed a primary election law. The law allowed the people to choose which candidate the party would nominate for the general election.

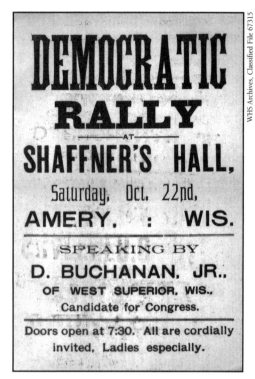

DEMOCRATIC RALLY

AT

SHAFFNER'S HALL,

Saturday, Oct. 22nd,

AMERY. : WIS.

SPEAKING BY

D. BUCHANAN, JR.,

OF WEST SUPERIOR, WIS.,

Candidate for Congress.

Doors open at 7:30. All are cordially invited, Ladies especially.

Democratic rally sign from many years ago

If more than 2 people want to run for the same office, then there is a primary election held in September. Voters choose to vote for candidates in either the Republican or the Democratic primary.

The 2 candidates who receive the most votes then continue on to the general election, held on the first Tuesday in November. In the general election, the candidate who receives the most votes is elected.

State officials—including members of the legislature, the governor, and other executive officers—are elected in the fall every other year. And county officials, like the county clerk and treasurer, also are elected in the fall. These, remember, are the partisan elections.

For example, there might be 3 Republicans running for governor, all of whom appear on the primary ballot. There might also be 4 Democrats whose names appear on the primary ballot. During the primary election in September, voters each pick the one candidate from their party whom they want to run for each office in the general election in November.

In the general election, only one Republican and one Democrat run for governor. Each candidate travels around the state to tell voters why he or she would be a better choice. On the first Tuesday in November, the voters go to the polls and vote for the candidates they think are best.

Rally for Republican Barry Goldwater, 1964. You can see signs both for Goldwater and against him.

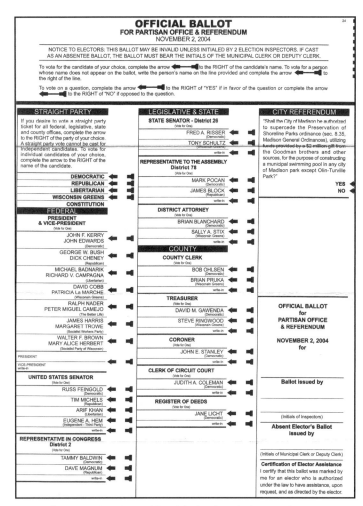

Ballot from the 2004 presidential election. Is it a partisan election? Check the ballot to find out!

Spring Elections

Spring elections are held every year. And the spring elections are non-partisan. In these elections, candidates may or may not be members of a political party. But they don't run as representatives of any political party.

Every spring, Wisconsin holds local elections and judicial elections. In local elections, voters choose a mayor, municipal officers, and members of the city council. They also choose a county executive and members of the county board of supervisors. Municipal elections and county elections are held every other year, since most officials serve 2-year terms.

The spring elections work just the way the fall ones do. People who want their names on the ballot need signatures from supporters.

And there is a primary in February if more than 2 people are running for the same office. A general election follows in April.

Some state officials are also elected in the spring. These include supreme court justices, judges, and the superintendent of public instruction.

Presidential Elections

Another kind of election is held every 4 years. It is both a spring election and a fall election. Every 4 years, voters in the United States choose a president. Every 4 years, many people want to be president and compete in state primary elections all over the country.

For example, there might be 8 Democrats running for president and 6 Republicans. This means there must be a primary election to select one Democrat and one Republican to run against each other.

Students hold a mock convention on November 2, 1968. Which candidates were running for president that year?

Wisconsin's primary is in the early spring. Wisconsin voters can only vote in one party's primary.

Voters decide whether they want the Democratic or Republican ballot. Then voters select one candidate on the ballot they have chosen. Candidates from smaller political parties, such as the Green Party, also run for office. And still other candidates are "independent." They run for office without representing a political party. They also do not need to run in the primary because they are not nominated by a political party.

Democratic State Convention ribbon, 1936
WHS Museum: 1972.54.1

Wisconsin is only one of the states that holds presidential primary elections. Following the spring primaries, each political party holds a convention during the summer. Each state sends delegates to the convention. If one candidate has won enough votes in primaries to have a **majority** (muh **jor** uh tee), the convention nominates him or her. If no candidate has a majority, the convention decides who will be the party's candidate.

The Wisconsin presidential primary determines whom Wisconsin's delegates will support. In November, these presidential candidates' names, as well as state officers' names, will appear on the Wisconsin fall ballot. Remember that fall elections are partisan. Wisconsin voters then get to choose both state and presidential candidates at the same time.

majority: More than half of a group of people or things; the number of votes by which someone wins an election

Looking Back

Parties and elections are an important part of how democracy works in Wisconsin. Parties nominate candidates for offices, educate voters on issues, and promote their candidates. People join political parties to help shape the parties' stand on important issues. Candidates elected from a party are expected to follow their party's ideas. Some political parties have been important in Wisconsin history: the Democrats, Whigs, Republicans, and Progressives. The Democrats and Republicans are important today. People also run for office as members of the Libertarian and Green Parties.

Wisconsin holds elections in the spring and the fall. Fall elections are partisan. Spring elections are non-partisan. Primary elections limit the number of candidates for the general election. And every 4 years when Wisconsin citizens vote in the presidential primary, they help select the candidate for president of the United States.

Chapter 8
Voices for Change

★ ★ ★

Do you ever have a hard time getting your teacher's attention? Or perhaps you once noticed a problem in your school that took a long time to get fixed. Similar things sometimes happen outside of school, too. You may have seen a streetlight that was burned out or a road that needed repair. In a democracy, we depend on our elected leaders to act when there are problems that threaten our rights or that make life unsafe or unfair. But sometimes these problems go unnoticed until someone reports that they need to be fixed. This is why it is so important to be active citizens. We must pay

Photo by Bob Queen, Wisconsin DNR

Students carrying cans to a recycling plant

attention to our community around us. Then we must figure out how to fix the problem and which elected leaders can help us make that change.

Adults who vote aren't the only people who can make positive changes in communities across Wisconsin and our nation. Young people need to get involved in pointing out problems and suggesting solutions. And your work *can* make a difference.

Questions to Think About

In what ways can students make positive changes in their schools and communities? How can they make sure that the issues they decide to work on belong to them and not to the adults advising them? Why are these responsibilities so important to ensuring the future of our democracy?

Our Communities/Ourselves

Throughout this book, you've compared and contrasted what happens within your family or classroom with the way government works. You've probably thought of other examples on your own. In this chapter, you'll read about students finding ways to carry out what they learned about how democracy works. There are many more examples of young people noticing things in their communities that needed improvement and working to make change happen.

In all of these cases, students realized that working to change things in their communities made living there better for them and their neighbors. And it was the students—not their teachers, parents, or other adults—who recognized what needed to change. And it was the students—again, not the adults—who figured out ways to accomplish their goals.

Students Organize for Change

Some adults in Waupun learned of a national program called Do Something, which helps students find issues *of interest to them* and problems that need to be fixed to make their community a better place to live. These adults helped organize a group of Waupun Middle School students who were ready to get involved. Do Something encourages students to take the lead in all things related to the project they choose. That is, students find a situation that needs improvement, then create and organize an action plan, and finally do the work to make sure that action is taken. The students want to see their hard work pay off in positive change.

One group of Waupun sixth-graders wanted to improve a railroad crossing near the school. The crossing was not well marked. Lots of brush was growing around it, making it very hard to see an oncoming train. The crossing was dangerous for the neighborhood around it and for those riding bikes or driving across it. Students decided to take their idea to the Waupun City Council. But when the students presented their idea at a meeting, members of the council told them that the council had to see evidence of the railroad crossing's danger.

Students had to come up with a way to conduct such an investigation. They decided that they would interview all the residents around the crossing to see how they felt. Almost every resident agreed that the crossing needed clearer markings to warn drivers.

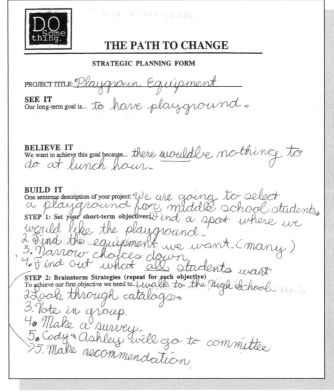

Do Something students organize to meet their goal of building a playground at their elementary school.

Office of the Commissioner of Railroads

Rodney W. Kreunen, Commissioner

610 N. Whitney Way
P.O. Box 8968
Madison, WI 53708-8968

Tel: (608) 266-7607
Fax: (608) 261-8220
TTY (608) 267-1479

February 23, 2000

Do Something League
Stephanie Spoehr, Advisor
Waupun Middle School
450 E. Franklin Street
Waupun, WI 53963

To The Do Something League:

Thank you very much for your letter regarding the Edgewood Drive crossing in Waupun. The information that you have put together shows that you are interested in a safe community, and also that my agency should do what we can to get answers for you. When we looked up the Edgewood Drive crossing records in our database, we learned that this crossing has some history. The City of Waupun filed a petition to build the street over the tracks on September 21, 1994. A hearing was held at Waupun on November 29, 1994. The Office of the Commissioner of Railroads issued its final decision on January 24, 1995. A copy of that decision is enclosed. I have also enclosed a copy of the record for the crossing from our database.

The order granted the city the new crossing over the tracks, required that a side track be moved, and also required that automatic flashing light signals be installed at the new crossing. The order notes that there were two to four trains daily at 25 mph. The railroad indicates that the train speed is now 30 mph. The order also notes that the city projected that 500 vehicles would cross this crossing each day. No actual count of traffic has been conducted. The signals were never installed. There are crossbuck signs, stop signs, and railroad advance warning signs at this crossing.

The reason that the signals were not installed has to do with the level of funding available for signal projects. The crossings with the most traffic get the funds for the new signals. The decision on where to spend the safety funds is made in part by comparing the exposure level of the crossings. The exposure is calculated by multiplying the number of trains per day times the number of vehicles. At Edgewood Drive, the 500 vehicles per day times the 4 trains per day produces an exposure of 2,000. The state generally considers signals when the exposure is 3-5,000 vehicles. At this crossing there are restricted views up and down the track, which makes the crossing less safe.

What I will do is to obtain a traffic count of the vehicles over this crossing. When that count is reviewed, we will be able to see what the actual usage is, and then be able to better decide what

signs or signals will be needed in the future. I will let you know what the traffic count turns out to be.

One other thing that we can do is to learn more about the safety of railroads and crossings. The Wisconsin Operation Lifesaver organization can be very helpful. They have speakers that visit schools and present information on rail safety. The Wisconsin contact person is Jim Tracey at 608 2677946. I have enclosed some information from the operation lifesaver website. You may want to see the Federal Railroad Administration website as well.

I want to thank you for bringing this rail-crossing problem to my attention. When I have further information I will let you know.

Sincerely,

Rodney W. Kreunen, Commissioner
Office of the Commissioner of Railroads

Enclosures

Then students wrote to the Wisconsin Commissioner of Railroads. When he replied, he told students that there should be automatic flashing light signals at such a crossing. But he wasn't sure that there was enough traffic to **justify** (**jus** tuh fy) the expense. He promised that his office would study the situation.

Students found out that things did not happen as quickly as they hoped, but they were able to achieve their goals. More than a year later, the study was completed. The railroad felt that the amount of traffic did not justify the flashing lights. Instead, a compromise solution was found. The railroad set up a series of warning signs and cleared out the brush. Because of the hard work of these students, the crossing is now safer.

Do Something students received this reply from the Wisconsin Commissioner of Railroads.

justify: Give good reason for

Photos by Stephanie Spoehr, Do Something

"Before" and "after" photos of the dangerous railroad crossing in Waupun

Other groups of Do Something sixth-grade students worked with the Waupun City Council, the Department of Natural Resources, and local property owners to get a bike path built to connect the city's Pine Street Park and the Fond du Lac County Park. The bike path provided a much safer route between the 2 parks. It was another project that made life better for the citizens of Waupun.

Now students in grades 3–5 at some other Waupun schools are signing up to be part of Do Something projects. Again, students choose the things that they want to improve for their school or larger communities. Some projects they want to accomplish, like buying new playground equipment, cost money. So the students organize ways to raise the funds. At Jefferson Elementary, Do Something students run a school store where classmates can buy school supplies and other small things once a week at morning recess.

Photo by Stephanie Spoehr, Do Something

2000-2001: Do Something students painting playground equipment at Jefferson Elementary, Waupun

WAUPUN — Since the inception of the Waupun Middle School Do Something League, the sixth grade members have targeted concerns within the community.

One of the concerns the group came up with was the railroad crossing on Edgewood and Woodland drives. There are railroad crossing signs at the crossing which require drivers to stop; however, students assert that very few people actually come to a full stop at the crossing.

Late last fall, a group of students spent a Saturday morning observing the crossing and surveying area residents. The students observed many cars crossing without stopping; sometimes without even slowing down and one who sped through at a high rate of speed. Going door-to-door, students talked with residents to get their feelings. Most residents had a safety concern with the crossing, noting most motorists just drive right through the crossing.

The students compiled the comments from neighbors and sent a letter to the state Railroad Commission expressing their concern. On Feb. 1, a group of students took their findings to the Waupun Department of Public Works. Representing the league were Justin DeMaa, Cameron Dary, Joey Pausma, Kyle Demers and Kyle Vande Zande, along with adviser Rich Dary.

Director of the DPW Scott Hermsen told the students, "A grant has been written asking for permission to erect lighted signals."

Mayor Harold Nummerdor addressed the students, telling them, "I have talked with the police department about this situation and asked them for their help as well. I agree this is a problem and that it will continue to grow next year. If we do not get permission for the lighted crossing this year, by next year we should have an even better chance to qualify for the signage."

Now, the students are concentrating on other concerns they have within the community.

Fond du Lac Reporter

Project Citizen is another national program where students take the lead in making decisions about creating positive change in their communities. At Heritage Christian School in West Allis, sixth-grade students choose one project a year. Similar to the railroad crossing in Waupun, one Project Citizen activity focused on a safety issue.

Students looked around the nearby neighborhood and realized there was a dangerous intersection with a 2-way stop. Many accidents or near-accidents happened at this busy spot. So students worked to convince the city council to install stop-and-go lights. They, too, investigated and presented their evidence at a town council meeting. Adults thanked the students for bringing the problem to their attention. The council members were also impressed that the students offered a solution. Although the town council did not put up expensive traffic lights, they did make the

Photo by Tracy Eastburn, Heritage Christian School

Project Citizen students present their ideas before a town council meeting.

intersection a 4-way stop. The city also put up lit warning signs that drivers could spot as they approached the intersection.

Students display window frames discovered while cleaning 9 area parks in Waupun.

Changes Take Time

In both of these cases, students did not get exactly the changes that they wanted, but they were able to work with elected leaders to make their communities safer places to live. Best of all, students did most of the work themselves. Now they understand how government works, and how young people can make a real difference when they make their voices heard.

Do Something and Project Citizen are 2 excellent ways to help communities. Why are they and projects like them so important to keeping democracy strong in Wisconsin? Students take the lead. They are the ones who go through the major steps in problem solving to make positive changes. First, they come up with an issue that they think can be changed. Then students organize an action plan for moving toward change. The next step is to make sure that the change they propose is something that others in the community want.

Remember that students in Do Something and Project Citizen had to do research and collect evidence to support their ideas. They worked hard to convince others. Most important, they did not give up, and they were willing to compromise. When the railroad would not put up automatic flashing light signals in Waupun, students were glad to see the brush removed and warning signs set

In Do Something's 2000-2001 "Pennies for Pals" campaign, Waupun's Jefferson Elementary students raised money for stuffed animals. The stuffed animals were donated to the Waupun police and fire department to calm frightened children at emergency scenes.

up. The students in West Allis did not get a stop-and-go light at the dangerous intersection, but a 4-way stop and warning stripes and signs that made the intersection safer were installed.

Jumping In with Strong Feelings

Students can make a difference in community decision-making, even without large and well-organized efforts. On January 31, 2005, the Madison School Board held one of the largest meetings in years. Earlier in the school year, the Madison School Board had adopted a **policy** (**pah** lih see) that would not allow classroom pets, because of their concerns about students with asthma and other allergies. Students in several elementary schools had strong feelings about changing that policy.

policy: Plan of action

Many second- through fourth-grade students came to the Monday night meeting to represent their interests by formally asking the school board to change their policy on classroom pets. According to the *Wisconsin State Journal,* Maureen Butler, a second-grader at Franklin Elementary, told the school board that the animals helped in science and taught students responsibility. Soleil Young, a fourth-grader at Randall Elementary, argued that pets offered students different kinds of learning opportunities. Other students offered their reasons for wanting classroom pets.

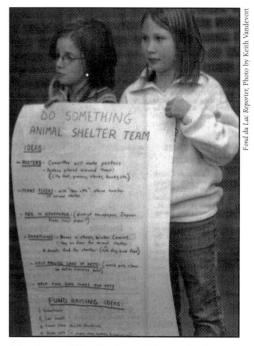

Fond du Lac Reporter, Photo by Keith Vandevort

The Madison School Board voted to allow classroom pets, provided that a pet caused no health problem to any student in a classroom. It was a great occasion for the students who attended the meeting, because their voices *did* make a difference.

Members of the Do Something animal shelter committee at Waupun's Jefferson Elementary School

Looking Back

Now that you've read *Voices & Votes,* you've learned a great deal about the way democracy works in Wisconsin. You know why sovereign nations have governments and that democracy is the form of government in which people choose their leaders. You found out that the United States and the state of Wisconsin both have written constitutions that tell us how government should work and explain the rights and responsibilities of citizens. Then you discovered why having 3 branches of state government—legislative, executive, and judicial—makes government more efficient *and* more democratic. Plus, you found that state government does all kinds of things to improve the lives of people in this state and that local governments work for people who live in counties, cities, villages, and towns. And you also learned how the governments of sovereign Indian Nations work.

You found out that a larger number of people are eligible to vote today than were able to do so when Wisconsin became a state in 1848, since women, African Americans, and American Indians were not allowed to vote back then. Although the Democratic and Republican Parties are now the largest political parties in Wisconsin, there were other parties earlier in our state's history, and there are smaller parties active in the state today.

In this chapter, you learned about 2 programs that try to get younger students involved in changing their communities—long before they are eligible to vote. And you found out that students can take action on an issue when they care about changing a policy. You are much smarter about democracy than you were when you started reading *Voices & Votes*, and you just might be ready to add *your* voice to your community. That's the way democracy works in Wisconsin, and you can be part of making it work better for all those who live here now and will live in our state in the future!

Glossary

abolish (ah **bahl** ish) Do away with

administrator (ad **mihn** uh stra tur) Someone who controls something

adopted (uh **dop** tud) Formally accepted and put into use

agencies (**a** juhn seez) Offices that provide services to the public

alder Representative

aldermanic (al dur **man** ic) Districts represented by an alder

alliances (a **li** un ses) Friendly agreements

amended Changed

appeal To ask that a decision made by a court of law be changed

appoints Chooses people for a particular job or duty

assembly (uh **sem** blee) One house of the state legislature

authority (uh **thor** uh tee) The right to do something or to tell other people what to do

ballot A secret way of voting, such as on a machine or on a slip of paper

bills Proposed laws

campaign (cam **pane**) A series of actions and activities, organized over time, to win something, like an election

candidates (**can** dih duts) People running for office

cede (seed) Give up

census (**sen** sus) When the government hires people to count everybody who lives in the United States

charges Blaming someone for a particular thing

circuit (**sur** cut) A circular path or route

circuit court (**sur** cut court) The lowest level trial court in the state judicial system

citizens (**sit** ih zuhnz) Members of a particular country who have the right to live there

commission (cuh **mih** shun) A group of people who meet to solve a particular problem or do certain tasks

compensation (com pen **sa** shun) Something that makes up for something else, such as a loss or injury

compromise (**com** pruh mize) To agree to accept something that is not exactly what you wanted

Congress (**cong** griss) Part of our federal government where laws are made

consensus (cun **sen** sus) Everyone consents or agrees

consent (cun **sent**) Agreement

constitution (con stuh **too** shun) In the United States, a written document that contains the rights and responsibilities people have and describes how their government will work

consumers People who buy goods or services

convention (cun **ven** chun) A large gathering of people who share the same interests

court of appeals The second level in the state judicial system

debate (duh **bate**) A discussion between sides with different points of view

debated Discussed from different viewpoints

defendant The person accused of breaking the law

delegates (**deh** luh guts) People selected to represent other people at a meeting

democracy (dih **mok** ruh see) A system of government which allows the people to choose their own leaders

democratic (dem uh **krat** ik) Where people choose their own leaders to represent them

Democratic Party One of the 2 major American political parties both historically and currently

discrimination (dis krim uh **na** shun) Unfair treatment of people, based on differences such as race, age, or place of birth

document (**dah** kyu muhnt) A piece of paper containing important information

efficient (uh **fish** unt) Working without wasting time

electors Those people who can vote

eligible (**el** uh juh buhl) Able or having the right qualifications to do something

enforce To make sure that a rule or law is obeyed

ensure To make certain that something happens

evidence (**ev** uh duhnts) Information and facts that help prove something or make you believe something is true

excluded (ex **clu** duhd) Left out

executes (**eg** zeh kyoots) Puts into action and enforces laws

executive (eg **zek** yuh tiv) **branch** Branch of government that enforces laws

executive (eg **zek** yuh tiv) The head of the state or the governor

exercise To use

Ezekiel (ee **zee** kee uhl) **Gillespie** An African American living in Milwaukee who was denied the right to vote

federal (**fed** ur uhl) A type of government where its smaller divisions—such as states—are united under and controlled by one government

finances Money

govern To rule

Green Party A modern American political party

House of Representatives One house of the Congress of the United States where states are represented based on the number of people living there

incorporate (in **cor** pur ate) When a large number of people, usually at least 1,000, living in a compact area decide that they need to provide more services and govern themselves with greater independence from the state or county

industrial (in **duhss** tree uhl) To do with businesses and factories

judgments Judges' solutions when people disagree on what the law means

judicial (joo **dish** uhl) **branch** Branch of government that settles arguments about interpretation of laws

justify (**jus** tuh fy) Give good reason for

La Follette, Robert M. (lah **fah** let) Man who helped form the Progressive Party

legislative (**lej** uh sla tiv) **branch** Branch of government that makes laws

legislators (**lej** uh sla turz) Lawmakers who make up the legislature

legislature (**lej** uh sla tchur) An elected group of people who have the power to make laws for the state

Libertarian (lib ur **tehr** ee uhn) **Party** A political party

licensing (**ly** suhn sing) Giving official permission to do something

majority (muh **jor** uh tee) More than half of a group of people or things; the number of votes by which someone wins an election

manufacturing (man yuh **fak** chur ring) Making something, often with machines

municipal (myoo **niss** uh puhl) To do with a city or town and its services, such as municipal workers

municipalities (myoo niss uh **pal** ih teez) Towns, villages, or cities

naturalized (**nach** ur uh lized) To become a citizen by studying and passing a test

nominates (**nahm** in ates) Suggests that someone would be the right person to do a job or to receive an honor

nomination (nahm uh **na** shun) Being chosen to run for office or to receive an honor or job

ordinances (**or** dih nun suhs) Laws issued by a governmental authority

override Cancel

partisan (**par** tih zun) To belong to one political party and agree with the views expressed by the members of that party

petition (peh **tih** shun) Request action from

platform Statement of what political party members think about the important issues of the day

policy (**pah** lih see) Plan of action

political (pah **lih** tih kuhl) Having to do with politics

politics The way a nation governs itself

population (pop yu **lay** shun) The total number of people living in a specific place

Progressive (pro **greh** siv) **Party** Party whose members supported progress or positive change

propose (pruh **poze**) Suggest

prosecutor (**pross** uh kyoo tur) A lawyer who represents the government in criminal cases

publish To produce and distribute a book, magazine, newspaper, or any other printed material so that people can buy it

ratify (**rat** ih fye) To agree or to approve officially

records (**rek** urds) Facts written down to keep as official documents

referendum (ref uh **ren** duhm) A vote by the people on a public measure

reform Working to change things for the better

regulations Official rules or orders

reject To turn down or vote against something

represent (reh pre **zent**) To speak for another person in government

representatives (reh pre **zen** tuh tivs) People chosen to speak or act for others

Republican (re **pub** luh cun) **Party** One of the 2 major American political parties both historically and currently

reservations (rez ur **vay** shuns) Areas that the Native people kept for themselves

reserved (re **zervd**) Kept

responsibilities (rih spon suh **bil** uh teez) Duties or jobs

rural (**rur** uhl) Having to do with the countryside or farming

senate (**sen** it) In the federal government one house of Congress where the states are represented equally. In state government, districts are represented equally in this house of government.

senators Those elected to serve in the senate

sessions Times when the legislature meets

sovereign (**sahv** rihn) A nation's right to rule itself and be completely independent of other nations

suburban (suh **bur** bun) Areas on the outskirts of cities with more homes than businesses

sued Started a legal case against someone in a court of law

suffrage (**suh** frahj) The right to vote

suffragists (**suh** frah jists) Women who led the fight for the right to vote

supreme court The highest level in the Wisconsin judicial system

surveying To determine the form, extent, and position of a piece of land by measuring

system (**sis** tum) A group of things that work in an organized way

taxes Money paid to the government

territorial (ter uh **tor** ee uhl) Having to do with a territory

territory (**ter** uh tor ee) A piece of land that belongs to the United States, but is not a state

tourism (**tur** izm) Travel for pleasure

treaties Official agreement between 2 sovereign governments

trial (**try** uhl) Trying or bringing a person to judgment in a court of law

trying Bringing to trial or to court

unconstitutional (uhn con stih **too** shun uhl) Against the rules described in the constitution

undemocratic (un dem o **krat** ik) Not very well representing the wishes of the people

union Another name for the federal government

universities (yoo nuh **vur** suh teez) Schools for higher education after high school. Universities are organized into colleges for different fields of study.

vacancies (**va** cuhn sees) Not occupied, as a job that is available

veto (**vee** toh) To reject a law

wards Places where people vote

Whig Party A historical American political party

zoning Keeping one area separate from another, such as businesses and houses

Manuscript Reviewers

Principal Reviewers

A. Peter Cannon
Madison

Kori Oberle
Madison

Content Reviewers

Teri Dary, President
Wave Action Team
Waupun

Tracy Eastburn
Heritage Christian School
West Allis

Alene Heeringa
Elementary Gifted & Talented
Teacher
Waupun Area School District

J. P. Leary, American Indian
Studies Consultant
Wisconsin Department of
Public Instruction
Madison

Kari Lindee, School
Psychologist
Waupun Area School District

Patty Loew, Assistant Professor,
Department of Life Sciences
Communication,
UW–Madison

Stephanie Spoehr, School
Counselor
Waupun Middle School
Waupun

Carol Taylor
School Counselor
Jefferson/Alto Elementary
Waupun

democracy it is! Advisory
Committee Educational
Communications Board

Tom Bobrofsky, Loyal
Elementary School, Loyal

Cathy Cullen, Carroll
College, Waukesha

Steve Doebel, Wisconsin
Public Television

Jo Egelhoff, Wisconsin
Taxpayers Alliance, Appleton

Peggy Garvey, Wisconsin
Educational Communications
Board

Randy Goree,
UW–Milwaukee, Milwaukee

Joyce Hemphill,
UW–Madison, Madison

Walt Herscher, Wisconsin
Council for the Social
Studies, Appleton

Andrea Isenbarger, Wisconsin
Educational Communications
Board

Kay Klubertanz, Wisconsin
Public Television

Hayden Knight, Cedarburg
High School, Cedarburg

J. P. Leary, Wisconsin
Department of Public
Instruction

Mike McKinnon, Janesville
Public School District,
Janesville

Sally Michalko, Waukesha
Public Schools, Waukesha

Clif Morton, New London

Kori Oberle, Wisconsin
Educational Communications
Board

John Robinson, Madison
Children's Museum, Madison

Dee Runaas, State Bar of
Wisconsin, Madison

Andy Soth, Wisconsin Public
Television

Paula Wick, Stoner Prairie
Elementary School, Verona

Classroom Reviewers

Tom Bobrofsky's and Barb
Kingsbury's fourth grade classes
Loyal Elementary School
Loyal

Jim Juech's, Julie Barnes's, and
Joanne Richards's fourth grade
classes
Saukville Elementary School
Saukville

June Shoemaker's and Vince
Kluth's fourth grade classes
Twin Lakes Elementary School
Twin Lakes

Ruth Weston's fourth grade
class
Emerson Elementary School
Madison

Paula Wick's fourth grade class
Stoner Prairie Elementary
School
Verona

Jill Puhlmann-Becker
Oakwood Environmental
Charter School
Oshkosh

Acknowledgments

Creating Voices & Votes would not have been possible without the wonderful work of Society editorial staff members Sarah Clement and Erica Schock, who worked tirelessly with the authors to find the visual materials that enliven the text and who reviewed and improved countless drafts of the text as well. Diane Drexler, with remarkable aplomb, kept the project on track.

Beyond the editorial facilitators, Andy Kraushaar, Harry Miller, and others in the archives and library helped unearth materials; Paul Bourcier, Leslie Bellais, and Joe Kapler from the Wisconsin Historical Museum gave us access to artifacts from the Society's collections, which Jay Salvo photographed; Jim Draeger from Historic Preservation identified significant courthouses throughout the state. Outside the Society, J.P. Leary from the Department of Public Instruction, and Patty Loew from the UW–Madison corrected interpretations and added insights into selections dealing with Wisconsin Indian Nations; Charles Rasmussen from Great Lakes Intertribal Fish and Wildlife Commission helped us find images and contacts in Indian Country; Bob Queen from the Department of Natural Resources and Ron Larson from Madison Newspapers provided access to and images from their collections; Kathleen Sitter from the Legislative Reference Bureau provided materials; Kori Oberle and Pete Cannon reviewed the entire manuscript for accuracy; Dee Runaas from the State Bar of Wisconsin led us to Project Citizen teacher Tracy Eastburn of Heritage Christian School in West Allis, who shared the works of her students; Teri Dary, Stephanie Spoehr, Carol Taylor, Kari Lindee, Alene Heeringa told us about the Do Something program; graphics designer of the entire New Badger History series Jill Bremigan gave the book its distinctive badgers and trademark look. Our spouses deserve special mention. My deepest appreciation to my ever-patient and dear Bill Malone who drove around the state helping tote materials to 4th grade classrooms for the "test drive" of the book and offered timely critiques of the manuscript whenever he was asked to do so. To Abby Markwyn, thanks for tolerating stacks of books on the floor and long soliloquies on reapportionment and territorial politics, and for being a wonderful friend and partner generally.

Index

This index points to the pages where you can read about persons, places, and ideas. If you do not find the word you are looking for, try to think of another word that means about the same thing.

Sometimes the index will point to another word, like this: Boats. *See* Ships. When you see a page number in **bold** it means there is a picture or map on the page.